# DEATH
## ON THE
# ICE

*The* Great Newfoundland
Sealing Disaster *of* 1914

CASSIE BROWN

*with Harold Horwood*

Anchor Canada

Library and Archives of Canada Cataloguing in Publication data is available upon request.

ISBN: 978-0-385-68506-1

Photographs courtesy of:
The Newfoundland Archives, Baine Johnston Company, Ltd., the Kean family and the Tuff family, the Cecil Mouland family, William C. Rolls, and from Cassie Brown's private collection.

Printed and bound in the United States of America

Published in Canada by Anchor Canada, a division of Random House of Canada Limited A Penguin Random House Company

Visit Random House of Canada Limited's website: www.penguinrandomhouse.ca

10  9  8  7  6  5  4  3  2  1

Penguin
Random House
ANCHOR CANADA

*To those members of the* Newfoundland's *crew who showed the human qualities of courage and heroism in the highest degree, and specifically to Jesse Collins, to Master Watch Arthur Mouland, to Cecil Mouland, and to John Howlett, this book is dedicated.*

L'Anse-aux-Mead...
St. Anthony
HARE BAY

STRAIT OF BELLE ISLE

GREY ISLANDS

WHITE BAY

CAPE ST. JOHN
Gull Island

NOTRE DAME
BAY

GULF OF ST. LAWRENCE

Ragged

Corner Brook

Stephenville

CAPE ST. GEORGE

CAPE ANGUILLE

Port-aux-Basques
Burgeo
CAPE
RAY

PLA...

CABOT STRAIT

ST. PIERRE
(FRANCE)

NEWFOUNDLAND

## AUTHOR'S NOTE

All the details of this story are true. The evidence given by fifty-two witnesses has been sifted and correlated from court records. We have reproduced as faithfully as possible the dialogue as it was remembered by the men who testified, or who later recorded their recollections of that unforgettable spring. Where testimony conflicts, both sides of the story are given, but we have often had to make a judgement as to what really happened. In a few cases, judgement must still be suspended.

Information was collected from files of the *Daily News*, the *Evening Telegram*, the *Mail and Advocate*, the Newfoundland Archives, and (with the kind permission of the former Attorney General of Newfoundland, the Hon. L.R. Curtis) the law library of Confederation Building, St. John's. Other sources include the Fisheries Research Board of Canada; the Meteorological Branch of the Department of Transport; C.F. Rowe, meteorologist; *Chafe's Sealing Book*: John Feltham: *Coaker and the F.P.U.*; J.R. Smallwood: *Coaker of Newfoundland*, and Abram Kean: *Old and Young Ahead*; Bertram H. Shears.

Cecil Mouland of Hare Bay, Bonavista Bay, and John J. Howlett of The Goulds supplied many details of the story in interviews taped in 1969 and 1970.

C.B.

St. John's

1972

# FOREWORD

Every spring for more than a century Newfoundland men and boys went out in ships to the most dangerous and brutal adventure that has ever been called an industry—the seal hunt. More than a thousand of them died when their ships sank, crushed like eggshells by colliding ice-fields, or exploded, or failed to pick them up from drifting floes, when boats were driven away in blizzards, or when those on foot were caught by storms. Survivors often lost fingers or toes, or sometimes feet or legs from freezing or other injuries.

The hardships they endured were compounded by the greed of the shipowners, who refused to provide clothing or safety equipment. The men had no meals to cook or any way to cook them: for weeks and months they lived on sea biscuit and tea. Even their drinking water was polluted with blood and seal fat until it stank. They slept like cattle in ships' holds without bedding. As the pelts and fat piled up, they simply lived on top of the cargo in utter filth. Injured men recovered as best they could, or died without medical help.

This book tells the story of the most appalling event in a long record of lost parties of sealers. The *Newfoundland* disaster, as it is called, was unique in several ways: It happened at a moment of reform—William Coaker, the workingman's hero of the time, was present as an observer on one of the ships to record the way the men were mistreated and the way the sealing laws were flouted by shipowners. As a result of the disaster the men rose up in revolt against feudal working conditions and against captains who valued seal pelts more than human lives; no less than two judicial enquiries sifted and recorded evidence from numerous witnesses; over it all brooded the patriarchal figure of Captain Abram Kean, the man chiefly responsible for the tragedy, and the only ice skipper ever to bring home a million seals.

A great uncle of mine, Sam Horwood, the master of a fishing schooner and as tough a man as I ever knew, was a sealer on Kean's ship that spring. Like others, he tried, ineffectively, to prevent the disaster, but he did not try hard enough. I once asked my father why someone as able and experienced as Sam Horwood did not lead a mutiny, if necessary, to save the lives of the sealers.

"Like all the rest of them, he was afraid of Abram Kean," my father replied. "The mutinies happened—but only after the men were already dead."

Though this book reads like a novel, it is historically accurate down to the last detail. Conversations between men on shipboard or on the ice-floes are reconstructed, word for word, from evidence given at the enquiries. Cassie Brown has done a remarkable job of research and reconstruction. She interviewed survivors at great length, studied all the written records and the meteorological and other data. The only liberty she has taken is to restore the dialect in which the men actually spoke, rather than give the "correct English" into which court reporters translated their speech.

This is Cassie Brown's book, not mine. She did more than nine tenths of all the work on it. My contribution was limited to editorial advice, mainly to cutting and trimming the narrative from a much longer one to its present length.

DEATH ON THE ICE is the most moving story I have ever read. I am proud to have had some small part in preparing it for publication.

HAROLD HORWOOD
TORONTO, 1972

To the Halifax *Chronicle* it was just a routine news item in the issue of May 11, 1914:

CHARLOTTETOWN, May 10—On Sunday morning a lobster fisherman employed at S.C. Clarke's factory at Bloomington Point on the north side of the island found the body of a man frozen fast in a floating ice cake about half a mile from land. Having nothing in his boat with which to cut the body loose from the ice, the fisherman had to abandon it; a heavy gale coming up, the boat had to make for land, and could not return to the body, which was carried out to sea. The dead man was evidently a sailor or fisherman judging by his clothing, and it is thought to be one of the Newfoundland sealers. . .

# CHAPTER ONE

On a black midnight, March 9, 1914, the S.S. *Newfoundland* ground her way through the loose ice of St. John's harbour heading for The Narrows and the ice-fields beyond. It was the old wooden steamer's forty-second year, the fourth as her captain at the seal hunt for twenty-nine-year-old Westbury Kean, the youngest son of the all-powerful Captain Abram Kean, unchallenged admiral of the sealing fleet.

The captain was young, but many of his crew were much younger. The dangers of the seal hunt, a spring ritual in which men slew and were slain, had made it the supreme test of manhood for Newfoundland boys. Lads of sixteen clamoured for "berths to the ice" and even fifteen-year-olds made the trip as stowaways.

One lad who had just turned sixteen slept legally in a wooden bunk in the *Newfoundland*'s hold. Albert John Crewe had talked his father into letting him make the voyage. The father, Reuben Crewe, now forty-nine, had sworn off seal hunting ("swiling") three years before after a harrowing experience at the ice.

"What, Reuben, ye goin' t'the ice again?" joshed a sealer who had met him on the docks. "I t'ought ye'd give up swilin' fer good."

"I come," Reuben stated soberly, "to look out fer Albert John, he were that set on swilin'."

The boy had got his "ticket" only because of his father's reputation. An old hand at the ice, he had been in the *Harlaw* on

April 7, 1911, when she was battered by a storm and crushed in the floes before sinking near infamous St. Paul's Island in the Gulf of St. Lawrence. Ten miles north-east of Cape Breton, this rock, two and three-quarter miles long, a mile wide, is ringed by perpendicular cliffs and chasms. Reuben and other *Harlaw* crewmen made it through the surf to the island, and somehow managed to scale the cliffs, but he had vowed never to hunt a seal again. Only anxiety for his son had made him change his mind.

One young man was on board under false pretenses. Signed on as "John Lundrigan" of Red Island, Placentia Bay, he was really Peter Lamb, of the same place. John had sold his "ticket" to Peter when he had a chance of a berth on the *Southern Cross*, which had sailed to hunt seals in the Gulf of St. Lawrence, on March 5. Peter had paid fifty cents for the ticket, and signed on under John's name, because the sale or exchange of tickets among sealers was illegal.

Not all sealers went to the ice with a light heart. Many of them were only too aware of the hazards of their calling. John Howlett, a well-set-up young man from The Goulds, ten miles south of St. John's, had suffered a chilling nightmare weeks before. In his dream he was on a mountain of ice, lost and freezing. He was alone, terribly and frighteningly alone, but everywhere he wandered there were vague, undefinable "things" on the ice around him—things with no particular shape that he could make out. He found himself walking among those things, unable to find his way, wondering what they were and dreading them. In his dream he was counting . . . counting . . . counting . . . He was still counting the white mounds when he awoke, shivering and terribly depressed. He had put the dream out of his mind, and now enjoyed untroubled slumber in the *Newfoundland*'s hold.

Wes Kean was not exactly in love with his old ship. To put it bluntly, she was a tub, ancient, under-powered, too long and too narrow to manoeuvre safely in an ice-field without danger of breaking in two. But he was a young man, with a name still to make for himself, and he had brought home a good voyage in her the year before, when the ice was loose and the seals plentiful.

But this year the ice was not loose. It was already giving him trouble as he manoeuvred northward from St. John's towards Cape St. Francis. The stuff he was butting was mostly "slob," small, roundish pans. Newfoundlanders distinguish between "local slob," usually too small to bear a man's weight, even when he is "coppying," or jumping from pan to pan, and "northern slob," formed off Labrador. Northern slob still consists of rounded pans, but larger, thicker ones that you can safely cross by coppying, provided you are careful to jump from each pan as it begins to sink under your weight. The ice the *Newfoundland* was butting now was mostly northern slob, some of it frozen into sheets and pans, and there was some ominous blue floe ice, from the Arctic, mixed with it.

Wes hoped the tightness of the ice was just local, caused by the north-east winds that had been driving it towards shore recently. Once he got north of Cape Bonavista, he hoped it might be looser, even though reports coming down from the north had not been encouraging. Ice had rafted against the land, layer piling on top of layer, at many points along the North-east Coast that year. It had damaged wharves and property and it looked like being a hard year at the ice. Still . . . if the wind came off from the west or sou'west, and blew a good breeze . . .

Wes, as ambitious as any other young captain to make good, had an additional incentive: his father. Abram Kean, or Captain Abe as he was generally called, was the commodore of the sealing fleet, already a legend at fifty-nine, with an unequalled record for getting seals. Of Devonshire stock, the Old Man was a tower of righteousness in a world constantly going to the devil. As a strict Methodist, he campaigned against liquor and advocated prohibition. His enemies accused him of intolerance, harshness, and a ruthless lack of regard for human life, particularly the life of common fishermen and sealers. But none of his enemies cared to say this in his austere presence; and none could point to a career so successful as his.

Born of an illiterate fisherman on a lonely island in Bonavista Bay, Abe Kean had somehow or other been born with ambition.

At first it was just the ambition to be skipper of his own vessel, the highest achievement a young fisher-boy in a remote part of Newfoundland could imagine. The youngest of the family, he was the only one sent to school, and then for only three years. At the age of eleven he had no trouble convincing his parents that he had all the book-learning a man of the world would ever need.

Only once in his life had his ambition wavered; at the age of ten, handling a gun, he shot himself in the hand and killed his three-year-old nephew. For months after that, shock and grief turned him into a recluse. But he recovered, and thenceforth had as stiff a backbone as anyone twice his age. At thirteen he turned his back on childhood, and went fishing and swiling. He married at seventeen, and fathered eight children. He also raised eleven others, the children of two older members of his family who had been struck down early by death.

He not only fed and clothed nineteen children until they grew up and married, and supported a disabled brother; he also sent his sons to school to the Methodist College in St. John's. Few indeed were the Bonavista Bay fishermen who ever managed to do that.

At seventeen he had sailed to the seal hunt in his brother's ship, and at twenty had been promoted to master watch, which meant he was in charge of an entire "watch" of sealers. A sailing ship might have two watches, a larger ship four. Later he had been promoted to second hand—the sealer' word for first mate—under another of his brothers.

His first year as skipper was a fiasco. At twenty-seven he had his first command, a barque belonging to a St. John's firm, which he took north to sail to the seal hunt. He got frozen in, and saw not so much as a seal's nose for the season. Next year, in command of the same ship, he saw her blown ashore and damaged. He quit sail and tried for steamers, but had to sign on as a minor officer to get a berth. The year after that—he was now thirty—he lost another ship, entirely through his own fault. But in spite of his record he was chosen by the Tory party to contest the Bonavista seat in that year's election. They needed a Methodist and a teetotaler. Kean amply fulfilled both conditions, and headed the poll. That same year he launched his own vessel (on a Friday, because he refused to believe in superstitions). No one in his right mind would launch a ship on a Friday, Newfoundlanders insisted—or begin any other important undertaking on that day. They were a superstitious lot. But Abe Kean believed in God and Abe Kean, nothing else. He seemed to be right, this time. That first year he landed a load of fish that must have been close to a record for a ship of that size. His luck had turned. His party leader, a big shipowner, also gave him his first command of a steamer at the seal hunt.

After that Abe Kean's career was a high road of success. With his first command in steam he made not only a full load, but the quickest "trip to the ice" on record—eleven days. He continued in the same ship until he lost her in the ice seven years later, he and his crew walking ashore. The owners did not mind. He was a driver and ships were made to be lost. What matter, so long as he got the seals? The following year he was made a Cabinet minister, and later given the Fisheries portfolio. It was the fist time a fisherman had risen to such a position in Newfoundland.

This was the man Wes Kean had to measure himself against—a record-setter, the greatest seal-killer who had ever "scunned" a ship through the ice from the lookout barrel at the masthead, the father of three sealing captains and two doctors, a determined man who, barely able to read and write, had gone back to school in his thirties, qualified himself in navigation, and passed exams for his master's certificate.

That year Captain Abe was in command of the *Stephano*, the biggest and fastest steel ship in Bowring's fleet of seven sealers. Regulations did not allow the steel ships to leave port for the hunt until March 13. The wooden steamers were allowed to leave their final ports (such as Wesleyville, where young Wes was headed) a day earlier. These dates applied to ships killing seals at The Front, north and east of Newfoundland. Those killing in the

Gulf of St. Lawrence were allowed to start a week earlier, for the seals of the Gulf herd had their pups a week earlier than those in the open Atlantic.

Wes Kean saw no seals on that run through the ice from St. John's to Wesleyville. All the seals were still off to the north, drifting slowly southward on the ice pack. But the ice did not slacken, as he had hoped. It took him almost three days to get to Wesleyville, in Bonavista Bay—a run that could be made in ten hours by a steamer in clear water.

# CHAPTER TWO

Nature had not been kind to Newfoundland. Surrounded by the hostile North Atlantic and attacked from the north by the frigid Arctic current, the island rises gaunt and grey out of a cold grey sea. The seventh largest island in the world, it is almost as large as Britain. But no gulf stream warms its rugged coastline; in that country of fogs and sharp breezes few men could scratch a living from the shallow soil. For many generations Newfoundlanders relied mostly on the sea.

Here Nature had been generous. The island's continental shelf, the Grand Banks, is the richest fishing ground in the world. It was the teeming silver shoals that brought the first fishermen here from Europe five centuries ago. Centuries earlier the Norse, those incredible seamen, had ventured into Newfoundland's coves and bays in the trading ships that they called "Knorrs." They settled for a while, but after bloody battles with the native Indians and Eskimos they sailed on. In the fifteenth century, hardy Basques came upon the Grand Banks and the island beyond. After that they came every year, using Newfoundland as a harbour and a base before they returned across the Atlantic, their holds full to the brim with fish and whale oil.

Sailors from other lands—from France, Portugal, and England—soon joined them. Fish were what they were all after, but the English gave the island its name and began to think in terms of colonies—the first royal patent for the founding of a colony there was given in 1502. Slowly the temporary harbour camps became permanent small settlements. Settlers—from the west of England, from France, from Scotland and from Ireland, seafaring men all—continued to trickle to the island and the settlements grew and expanded. But it was a harsh life, a constant struggle for survival. The men fished; the women grew what vegetables they could, and raised some sheep, goats, and poultry. The only other meat was what they got by gun or snare—ducks, geese, rabbits and, in hard times, sea birds. In bad fishing seasons families starved.

For two centuries these self-reliant people lived almost entirely in the Avalon Peninsula in the south of the island where St. John's, the main town, was situated. But as the population spread northward through Bonavista and Notre Dame bays in the early 1700's they discovered a new source of supplies, an additional resource to fishing, hunting, and subsistence farming.

Seals! Millions of seals floating by the northern part of the island, lying on the ice-field that was slowly being swept out to the Grand Banks.

For thousands of years, these harp seals had completed their annual migratory circle from the Arctic to the Grand Banks and back again. The herds spent their summers in Hudson Bay and Davis Strait, on the west side of Baffin Bay, and far to the north in Lancaster Sound. They began moving south ahead of the ice when it began to form in late summer, and by the first of November were off the northern tip of Labrador. Here they met the herd of much larger hood seals; they had crossed from Greenland and would remain close to the harps until they reached northern Labrador again, early the following summer. The hoods were much less numerous than the harps and remained always two or three miles south-eastward from the main harp herd.

At the Straits of Belle Isle, the harp herds split, one herd swimming down the east coast of Newfoundland, the other swimming through the Gulf of St. Lawrence, but both herds disappearing at sea somewhere to the south of Newfoundland. They would not be seen again until February, when they might be sighted off southern Newfoundland, swimming northward to meet the ice in the Gulf and at The Front.

There the harp mothers climbed up on the ice pans in dense herds. In early March they gave birth to their pups, hundreds of thousands of the young seals all being born on the ice within a week. The male harps were off at the floe edge enjoying themselves, or mingling in an offhand manner with the herd. They did not stick close to the females at this season. The females did not feed at this time either. They drew on their stored body fat and gave a fat-rich milk for the whitecoats—so rich, indeed, that the young ones' weight would double in a week.

As the pioneer settlers pushing to the north of Newfoundland discovered, these fat young whitecoats were easy prey, since neither the male nor the female seals usually remained to defend their young. Even if there was open water nearby the young seals could not yet move to it or swim in it. They simply lay where they were while the men scrambled over the ice to them and dispatched them with a blow to the nose. It was much easier than the old way of catching individual seals in nets set in the water—a practice still common among the white settlers of Labrador. It was not very "sporting" hunting—clubbing fluffy, white baby seals with big, black helpless eyes—but that thought had no place in the mind of a hungry man with a hungry family on the shore.

The seal meat proved to be rich food. The unpalatable parts could be fed to the dogs. The hides, the hunters soon found, made splendid leather for boots and clothing. The fat, rendered into oil, fed their lamps and made excellent soap. A new industry was born.

Then in skiffs and shallops the Newfoundlanders soon began to nose around the ice-field looking for seals. Even with simple boats like those they were able to produce a surplus of hides and fat. These the shrewed St. John's merchants kindly took off their hands and then sold at fancy prices on the world market. But it was not until the closing years of the eighteenth century that the first sailing ship was fitted out to seek a load of seals.

By 1804, the sealing fleet numbered 140 vessels, all under 30 tons. By 1840, there were 631 such small sealers, and the big barques, brigs and brigantines were beginning to take an interest. In 1857, no fewer than thirteen thousand Newfoundlanders went in sailing vessels to the seal hunt.

By the 1850's, they were landing more than half a million seal pelts a year—half a million in a season measured in weeks, not months—and the merchants were growing rich. It was a terrible business in which men lived and worked like dogs, sacrificed their ships as a matter of course, and often died on or under the ice pans. More than a thousand Newfoundlanders lost their lives in this desperate adventure. No one ever counted the sailing ships that went down.

It was the ice that sank the ships, the ice that killed the men. For the ice-field on which the sealers had to work was a treacherous, ever-shifting enemy, the delinquent offspring of many strange and powerful forces.

The ice-field begins in late summer as young ice in Baffin Bay. Slowly it moves south. In November off Labrador the sea is dappled by small circular pieces of ice that have been chopped and crushed to a snowy consistency by wind and sea. Under winter's encouragement this grows rapidly into blocks six to ten feet in diameter, a lively translucent green with white edges created by constant grinding against other pans. This is known to mariners and sealers as slob ice. On calm winter nights off the Labrador coast the sea freezes until these blocks are embedded in large sheets of ice that may be several miles in length, but are constantly forming and reforming under pressure of sea and wind. This becomes the sheet ice that is the home of the whelping seals.

Meanwhile, the Polar Pack (the ever-present ice of the Arctic) presses southward behind the local ice. Its heavy floes are blue and as much as five feet thick. It is dense ice, frequently covered with gravel, mute testimony to its assaults upon the land on its southward journey. It is rugged, jagged, and altogether intimidating.

By the time the Polar Pack has joined it, the ice-field presents a formidable barrier to ships. It is not simply a flat coating of ice on the surface of the ocean. Far from it. Every year on the journey south strong north-east winds drive the ice-field tight to the land; when the pressure becomes too great, huge pans of ice buckle, crack, and rear out of the sea, jamming against one another to form "pressure ridges" like small mountain ranges. For miles the ocean is loud with the crackling and roaring of ice pans rafting on other ice pans. Ice-floes slowly turn turtle and are nipped by other floes and held in that position.

It is with this constantly moving, splitting, wheeling, cracking, roaring jagged mass of ice that the sealing skippers had to contend, working their way slowly towards the seals as openings appeared, allowing ships to remain jammed for days at a time when the ice was tight, always taking their chances on being crushed and sunk.

The first steamers headed into the ice pack in 1863. Of the first fifty wooden steamships that went sealing between that year and 1900, no less than forty-one were lost at sea. But by the time they joined the hunt the seal herds were already decimated, and despite their power and manoeuvrability they rarely managed to equal the half-million kills of the sailing ships.

In the early 1900's, the first steel ship joined the sealing fleet. She was the *Adventure* built to the specifications of a St. John's merchant, Alick J. Harvey, so that she was the first ice-breaker in the world. The other Newfoundland merchants, impressed by the new steel ship, began adding their own steel ships to the fleet of "woodenwalls." By 1914, Newfoundland was the only country in the world with a fleet of ice-breakers.

Men like Alick Harvey were the real rulers in Newfoundland, not the King in far-off England, not the English governor, not even the Upper and Lower Houses of the Legislature in St. John's. The aristocracy of the island, the merchant families of Water Street, had first made their money from trade in fish and later from trade in seal hides and fat. These profits had enabled them to branch out in other fields—buying steamship lines and so on—until all contact with the outside world seemed to be through them. Many of these merchants had import and export links with as many as fifteen foreign countries.

On the island they ran everything. They ran the fisheries, the shipping lines, the seal hunt; it seemed that every time money changed hands on the island it rolled inevitably into their tills. Not that money did change hands very often; the St. John's merchants controlled all of the communities outside the town through the outport merchants who bought on credit and sold on credit, perpetuating the system that held the fishermen in bondage. It was as if the entire island was a "company town" and every store a company store—with the men of Water Street quite content to keep things that way.

While the wealthy merchants lived in mansions in St. John's and sent their children to the best public schools in England, the children of the fishermen hardly knew what schooling was. At the age of ten they were fishing in open boats with their fathers; at fourteen they were men who knew they could expect hard unceasing labour and bitter poverty to the end of their days. They would see little cold hard cash in their lifetime, since they would usually be in debt to the local merchant, who gave them barely enough credit to feed and clothe their families during the long winter months. If the spring and summer fishery had been fruitful, the merchant decided on the price he would pay for the fish, wiped the debt off his ledger, and granted the fishermen the privilege of remaining on his books. If the harvest had been really bountiful and there was actual *cash* due to come to the fishermen, they were often persuaded to let it remain on the books on the credit side of the ledger. The merchant then sold the fish to the fish-hungry countries overseas at enormous profit and the money rolled in.

That was the system. The fishery brought greater wealth to the wealthy and a bare existence to the masses. Because generation after generation was born to poverty and incredible hardship and died in the same circumstances, the fishermen accepted the system. They were a hardy, manly breed. The sea moulded their existence and the sea moulded their character. Like seamen everywhere they were daring, foolhardy, superstitious, religious, outstandingly brave; and thanks to their bleak life at home and their early experience at work, they were able to withstand great privation.

That last quality was important. It meant that they actually looked forward to the seal hunt. Early each February all over the island fishermen pricked up their ears when they heard that the old wooden sealing ships (lying along the waterfront at St. John's) were being prepared for the annual seal hunt in March.

The eager seal hunters knew what they were heading for—a terrible voyage, living and working like dogs, their arms constantly caked with blood up to the shoulder, short of sleep, and with little time to do more than snatch a bite to eat, and working, constantly cold, on heaving, cracking sheets of ice that could give way under them or break off and float away with them into the icy darkness—they knew all this, but they cheerfully flocked into St. John's to volunteer, in fact to compete, for tickets to berths on the ships going "to the ice." This was their one chance to earn hard cash. And besides, what else was there for a fisherman to do in Newfoundland in March?

There was another reason. For Newfoundlanders, the seal hunt had a significance even beyond its cash value. Theirs was the only sealing fleet in the world, commanded by captains who were national heroes, and in great demand as ice pilots for polar expeditions. Men like Robert Peary might reap the international renown, but it was the Newfoundland sealing captains who guided their ships through apparently solid fields of ice to within five hundred miles of the North Pole itself.

Whatever their reasons, in the harsh winter of 1914, men left their outport homes and came flocking to St. John's, eager to find a berth to the seal hunt. They came any way they could. Those who could afford it came by train, but most arrived by horse and sleigh, or on foot. To the townspeople they looked strange; poorly dressed in rough worn clothing, their legs encased in clumsy home-made sealskin trousers with boots of rawhide or sealskin on their feet, gunny sacks slung over their shoulders, sculping knives belted around their middles.

Into St. John's they came, trudging through snowdrifts; tough, raw boned, their faces seamed by constant exposure to the biting winds. Before their ships sailed, there would be fifteen hundred of them, not in the least intimidated by the condescending attitude of the townspeople, sophisticates fresh from the Casino Theatre's performances by the W.S. Harkins touring repertory company.

All the while the grey little town resounded to the squalling of winches and cranes and the shouts of seamen as the ships were outfitted and prepared—stripped to a skeleton to make room for every last seal pelt—in readiness for the seal hunt.

# CHAPTER THREE

When Wes reached Wesleyville, where he had arranged to pick up the rest of his crew, he found that the "old hands" there were forecasting a disastrous year. The ice was too tight for the ships to work, they said. They doubted that the steamers would even get out of the harbour after picking up the sealers waiting there for berths. There was some reason for their gloom. That winter was already being called "the winter of storms," and almost every week there were reports of ships lost at sea or missing with all hands.

The sealers themselves were optimistic. They always were. Only incurable optimists would face the odds of the ice-floes in the first place. Every year, every sealer expected that *his* ship would find "the Main Patch," as the big herd was called.

By 1914, of course, everyone, even the incurable optimists, knew that the great herds of the past were gone. In recent years the annual crop of whitecoats had averaged no more than 200,000. But everyone knew, too, that when a ship was "burned down in the fat" or stopped right in the middle of the main herd, there was money to be made. Crews didn't take long to kill large numbers of seals. It was simply a matter of walking among the two-week-old whitecoats, killing them with a tap on the nose, then quickly flipping them over, slitting them open with sculping knives, and separating hides and fat from the carcasses. Only hides and fat were considered of any value, so the bloody carcasses were left littering the ice. Working quickly a crew would easily kill and skin five or six thousand seals in a day. With that sort of luck—so every sealer dreamed—they would have a good chance to match or better the "crew's share" of $148 that Captain Abe's crew had made in 1910 before their crop was deducted.

The crop was the equipment that every sealer had to have. It was supplied by the shipowners, up to a total of $15, and deducted from his earnings. Thanks to the crop, sealers sometimes ended the season in debt to the owners of the ships, for only one third of the nominal value of the catch was divided among the three hundred or so members of a crew. This nominal value had no relation to market value, however. It was set, arbitrarily, at a meeting of the shipowners, the firms who "owned" the seal hunt. But that fantastic bill of $148 stuck in men's minds. They forgot that the *average* earnings on Captain Abe's ships (the most successful, on the average, at the hunt) were only $29 a year, averaged over his twenty-nine years as master, after the crop was deducted. The sealers lived on hope. But they had plenty of that.

From the northern part of the island they came trudging into Wesleyville through the snowdrifts or riding on "catamarans" drawn by horses, men whose language kept the strange words of the Devon and Cornwall dialects of Shakespeare's day. A few of them came by dog team from far to the north in Notre Dame Bay. These were men of the north, fishermen who tried to keep their families in food by hunting ducks and geese in summer and autumn, and caribou, hares, and ptarmigan in winter. Like their southern shipmates they were dressed in short jackets of tough cotton weave, little of their clothing was made of wool—the only fibre that could protect a man properly on the ice-field. On their feet were home-made boots, the only kind most of them ever owned. Made of sealskin or rawhide, they were good enough in dry snow. But they soon soaked through when they got wet, as they often did when used among loose ice pans.

Most of the men had tickets, issued in advance, giving them the right to their berths. Others came "on spec." One by one they "signed on," marking an "X" after their names on the ship's register, for very few could write their own signatures.

From Doting Cove, thirty-five miles to the north, came a happy group of teen-agers, proudly presenting their tickets for their first trip to the ice. They were Cecil Mouland, his cousin Ralph Mouland, William and Daniel Cuff, David Abbott, Phillip Abbott, and Art Mouland—no relation to the Arthur Mouland, one of the four master watches, already on board.

The men were divided into four watches under Arthur Mouland, Thomas Dawson, Sidney Jones, and Jacob Bungay. Cecil Mouland and most of his group ended up in Bungay's watch, for he was the youngest officer, and the others had their pick of the more experienced men.

Cecil, a cheerful, smiling lad and the leader of his little group, was filled with love for the girl he had left behind him—Jessie, a young schoolteacher whom he had already vowed to marry. He was also filled with good advice from his grandfather. "Cecil," the old gentleman had warned, "if ever ye gets caught out on the ice be sure to keep yer face in motion. Chaw on something all the time, an' that way yer face will never frostburn." Cecil had no intention of being caught out on the ice, of course, but he also had no intention of returning to Jessie with parts of his face missing, so he took his grandfather's advice seriously, and carried, stowed about his person, a number of plugs of chewing tobacco—it never hurt to be prepared.

The master watches were top dogs on the ice, each in charge of his quarter of the ship's crew. On board, they were all subject to the second hand, who ranked next to the captain. In the *Newfoundland* this was George Tuff, a sealer with seventeen years' experience, though he was only thirty-two. He had served for ten years as a master watch, the last three under Wes Kean. This was his first as second hand. Rising from the ranks like this—from the very bottom—he had to be a very fortunate man indeed.

None understood his fortune better than George Tuff. At sixteen he had gone to the ice "for a lark," and made a little bit of money—enough to coax him back another year. That year, 1898, he signed on the S.S. *Greenland* and was caught in one of the grimmest sealing disasters in history, when forty-eight men, trapped on the ice by a wheeling pressure ridge and a break in the ice-field, had frozen to death. For Tuff, months of nightmare followed, during which he saw dead sealers rising from open water between the ice pans and walking towards him, until he woke up screaming. The horror never quite left Tuff. But seventeen-year-olds recover quickly, and next year, desperately short of money, he went to the ice again.

He went back year after year until he no longer thought of staying ashore. He had worked well and earned well-deserved recognition, particularly from the Old Man, who let it be known that he considered George Tuff a good hand.

Also on board the *Newfoundland* was a navigating officer, Captain Charles Green, placed there by law because Wes Kean did not have a master's certificate. Green was an experienced ice skipper, who had spent many years in the Arctic. But he was explicitly told by the owners, Harvey and Company, that he was to have nothing to do with the running of the ship. At most, the navigating officers were there to give the sealing captains advice if and when they asked for it. Captain Green and Wes Kean rarely exchanged more than the formal courtesies.

They spent their second night in Wesleyville while a northeast storm raged. In company with the *Eagle* the *Newfoundland* cleared for the ice-field at 8 A.M., March 12. The wind had come from the north and was sweeping the ice around Cape Freels with unusual violence. They passed Flowers Island (the ancestral home of the Keans) about three miles off shore, and fought their way to Cabot Island, five miles farther, off the cape. They could not buck the ice flowing southward, so they hove to in the lee of Cabot Island and dropped anchor. They were joined shortly thereafter by the *Sagona*.

Their position was far from safe. Cabot Island has no real anchorage and offers little shelter. The three captains conferred by signals, and decided to retreat to Flowers Island—actually two islands with a harbour between them. Here there was good anchorage, and here they spent another night. It was a poor beginning for a sealing voyage.

As night advanced, two stowaways were found and brought before Wes. With a fine show of anger he lectured them, then sent them to work with the firemen for their keep. He'd get full value out of them as stokers. But stowaways were regarded as bad luck by the crew.

At dawn the wind had died down, the ice had slackened, and the three ships made it around Cape Freels, the sturdy *Eagle* and *Sagona* breaking the way of the graceless old *Newfoundland*.

Just as the wooden ships were getting under way at Flowers Island, the steel fleet was preparing to sail from St. John's. Built for the seal hunt they were large, powerful ships with hulls specially shaped to allow them to run almost their full length on top of the ice, crushing it with their sheer weight.

The *Stephano*, under Captain Abram Kean, was considered the most powerful, but she had close and worthy rivals in the *Florizel* under Captain Joe Kean, the Old Man's eldest son, *Beothic*, under Captain Billy Winsor, a young and brash ice skipper who was giving the Old Man a run for his money nowadays, and in the *Nascopie* under Captain George Barbour, a very able and experienced sealer who made good voyages even though he put the safety of his ship and his men above the desire to be "highliner" for the year.

The other steel ships, the *Adventure*, the *Bonaventure*, and the *Bellaventure*, were older, but were still able ice-breakers. Traditionally, there was great excitement in the town as the fleet cast off and raced for The Narrows. But the year before, two of the ships had collided in The Narrows in the race to be first into the ice, so now, by arrangement, the three old ships sailed first, followed by the *Nascopie*, the *Beothic*, the *Florizel*, and lastly the *Stephano*. Though the Old Man was last to leave, the betting was heavy that he would be the first around Cape St. Francis. He wasn't, in fact, but he was first around Cape Bonavista, the next point northward, and by 7 P.M. he had led the fleet into the heavy slob east of The Funks, and was burned down for the night. He was not only north of the ice-breakers, but was also close to the wooden steamers that had left Wesleyville that morning.

The *Nascopie*, trailing Kean's *Stephano* in the ice, had a very special passenger that year. His name was William Coaker. Like Captain Kean, he had started from nothing. But whereas Kean had made his mark as the servant of the establishment, the driver who got the seals for the merchants, Coaker had risen to become one of the most powerful men in the country solely as leader of the fishermen. He had founded and edited a tough radical newspaper, *The Fishermen's Advocate*, and he had formed the fishermen into a union "forty thousand strong." He and a group of associates ran for the House of Assembly in 1913 and won. In the House they defiantly wore their roll-necked blue guernseys, the badge of the fishermen's revolution. Now he was making this voyage to see that the ill treatment to which the sealers had been traditionally subjected was not continued.

That year, as leader of the Fishermen's party in opposition in the House of Assembly, he had introduced his Sealing Bill, calling for decent food, full-time cooks, and other crumbs of civilization on board the sealing vessels. The government had fought and stalled for months, introduced amendments, and amendments to the amendments, and debated until it looked as if they were going to "talk out" the Sealing Bill altogether. But they knew this would alienate the fishermen's votes in the few fishing districts where they still had some strength, so reluctantly, on the day before the steel fleet sailed, the last day the Legislature sat, they allowed the bill to go through—too late to affect the wooden ships, but in time to bring the ice-breakers within the law.

Coaker's passage to the ice was arranged with Job Brothers, owners of the *Nascopie*, and it was certain that on this ship, if on no other, the Sealing Law would be enforced. For Coaker was a truly remarkable man, a savage fighter who took no nonsense from anybody, and had tens of thousands of fishermen at his back, well organized into his Fishermen's Protective Union.

Besides the union, he had the Fishermen's Union Trading Company, powerful enough to challenge established firms like Job's, Bowring's and Harvey's. He had his newspaper, and he had his Fishermen's party, which often held the balance of power in the House of Assembly.

The merchants, who had always ruled the roost in Newfoundland, and kept the fishermen in a state of absolute serfdom, found themselves forced to compromise with Coaker. They had to allow him to force through his reforms, to treat him with respect, even to accept his advice. Otherwise he might have made good his threat to capture a majority in the House of Assembly and install a Fishermen's government—a prospect too dreadful to be contemplated.

Coaker kept a most meticulous log of the voyage, in which he recorded not only most of the incidents of the hunt, but also his thoughts and reflections on it. He was planning to use it as political ammunition in the years ahead, when he would make his bid to become Prime Minister.

On the decks that day the sealers were busy fixing steel hooks to light poles, the "gaffs" that they would use to kill whitecoats, and that they also carried for safety. If a man fell through the ice, as he often did, he could usually get out with the help of his gaff. If he had any trouble, another sealer came to his aid with the hooked gaff. The gaffs were also used to handle the pelts, up to the time they were attached to the towing ropes to be hauled to the ship.

On Saturday, March 14, at 8 A.M., the men of the *Newfoundland* saw their first seals—scattered families of hoods. They did not stop to hunt them. Hoods were big, dangerous animals who stayed in family groups, and a dog hood would fight for his mate and pup. He could easily kill an inexperienced sealer. Anyway, they were not interested in hoods so long as they could make progress northward towards the main herd of harps. But the hoods were a welcome sign. Within hours, most likely, they would be "in the fat."

By 10 A.M., Wes Kean could see his father's ship approaching, with the rest of the steel fleet strung out behind him. By noon both the *Stephano* and the *Florizel*, the latter skippered by his elder brother Joe, had passed him.

Wes would have liked to exchange messages with the other ships, but could not do so because the *Newfoundland* had no wireless. All the steel ships were equipped with the new-fangled device (Marconi had flown his famous kite near St. John's and received the historic wireless signal only thirteen years before). But the *Newfoundland* had been stripped of her wireless set because, according to the owners, Harvey and Company, it was not paying for itself. A wireless was supposed to get you more seals, but the set on the *Newfoundland* had proved a disappointment in this respect. The owners wanted it out, so it came out.

Wes had talked about it with his father, while still in St. John's, and they had agreed on a signal that could be seen as far away as a ship was visible through the spy-glass.

Wesbury, me b'y," the Old Man had said, "kape as handy to me as ye can, an' when we reach the swiles I'll let ye know be raisin' the after derrick. Now when ye see the after derrick ris, ye'll know we're in the fat." He bent a thoughtful blue eye on his youngest son, and stroked his white beard. "Now if ye happen to get to the swiles first, Wesbury, me b'y, ye'll let me know be h'isting yer stays'il."

So it had been agreed. This sort of deal between members of the same family was not regarded as dishonourable, even though they were working for competing firms, the Old Man for Bowring's, Wes for Harvey's.

But as Wes saw the *Stephano* disappearing to the northwest he thought, ruefully, that by the time he caught up with the fast ice-breaker most of the swiles might already be in her holds. He envied his brother Joe, whose fine, fast *Florizel*, an ice-breaking passenger ship stripped for the voyage, had no trouble keeping the Old Man in sight.

All the other ice-breakers took care to keep him in sight, too. For their captains were convinced that if anybody found the seals it would be Abram Kean. Nine years out of ten he was first into the fat.

Wes quietly cursed his lack of wireless and turned back to the job of navigating the *Newfoundland* through the thickening ice-field. It was giving him more trouble than he liked. He didn't need wireless to tell him that the ice was tight to the land, and that there was no chance of taking the "inside run" where the water was often clear. There was no way he could get into either Fogo Harbour or Seldom-Come-By where he was supposed to be picking up the last of his crew. He decided to leave them, and headed north-west forty men short-handed. They were still among the hoods when he burned down for the night. Far off, but still in sight, the steel fleet had run into heavy ice and was forced to burn down also.

Coaker, in the midst of the close-packed fleet of ships, re-corded in his log that night that it looked more like a city than the open Atlantic. The white ice-field stretched solidly in every direction, and the lights of big ships everywhere burned brightly.

On Sunday there was a fresh breeze from the south-west, the ice slackened, and the *Newfoundland* found herself, shortly after dawn, steaming through "lakes" of clear water. But by 10:30 A.M. the ice had closed, and brought her to a halt. Around her, scattered seals bawled and played, but no one would think of killing seals on a Sunday. Tomorrow, they promised each other, they would have bloody decks and a meal of flippers in the night. They licked their lips hungrily. They had been living mainly on hard tack and black tea since leaving St. John's eight days before. The hard tack was ship's sea biscuit made out of flour and water without any kind of leavening. The oval cakes were about three inches thick, and so hard you had to break them with a hammer and then gnaw at them. To men who had starved on this diet—almost nothing else, for eight long days—the thought of fresh seal meat was almost maddening.

By contrast, Coaker reported in his log that the *Nascopie*'s crew were happy with their meals, which, no doubt thanks to

Coaker's note-taking presence, included fresh beef for Sunday dinner. They had spent the day in communal hymn-singing.

Meanwhile, the steel fleet had left the *Newfoundland* out of sight, somewhere to the south-east.

On Monday, the *Newfoundland*, unable to make any worthwhile progress, put her men over the side to kill hoods. The seals had scattered during the night, and were hard to find. Many an ice party had a long haul over the floes with only a few pelts. But by night they had, indeed, "bloodied their decks," and had seal meat in the stew pots.

The men had to do their own cooking. The only full-time cook worked for the officers, cooking their food—which included fresh beef, reserved exclusively for their use. The "cooks" employed for the men were required to kill and stow seals, like the others, and had little equipment to cook with, even if there had been galley space to prepare meals for hundreds of sealers, which there wasn't. Most of the cooking was done in the holds, over tiny coal stoves called "bogies." Even this would be abandoned later, and the men would be forced out of their wooden bunks, too, as the holds filled up with pelts and their attached thick layers of fat. Late in a successful voyage the sealers would simply sleep on top of the bloody, greasy cargo without removing even their coats, and would try to satisfy their hunger with cold hard tack and melted snow, or occasionally with raw seal meat. Many of them learned to eat the warm, fresh hearts cut still beating from seal carcasses. The squeamish, who had a horror of hot blood and live muscle in their mouths, soon learned to overcome it. Like the polar bears, which were seen occasionally on the ice-field and which also depended on seals for life, they soon came to relish the taste of live meat.

On St. Patrick's Day, March 17, the fleet of ice-breakers was tightly jammed, and the ships were so close together that the crews visited back and forth from ship to ship. Learning that their hero, William Coaker, was on board the *Nascopie*, some of the men carried complaints to him about the lack of decent meals and the absence of cooking facilities. In fact, the ships were ignoring the new Sealing Law. By a strange coincidence Coaker's ship, the *Nascopie*, was the only one obeying it.

Coaker promptly sent a wireless message to the owners, warning them that they could be sued unless they acted to remove the complaints. The crew on board his own ship never had it so good.

The official day for seal killing to begin had been March 15, but on St. Patrick's Day the ice-breakers were in such heavy ice that four of them—*Stephano, Nascopie, Beothic* and *Bellaventure*—had to co-operate closely in one small area in an effort to break themselves free.

Under their concentrated power, the ice at last gave way. They seemed to be on the verge of success, then the ice buckled and began to raft. Huge fragments went skidding over the surface to pile up with a thunderous noise against the ships' sides. The *Nascopie* was nipped by the rafting ice and held fast. The other three hastily went astern, and the *Beothic*'s port quarter collided heavily with the *Stephano*'s starboard quarter, denting her plates and frame and damaging her staterooms.

Ah! Bad luck for the Old Man.

It took dynamite—always a risky business, but often necessary—to free the *Nascopie*, and it was not until evening that they finally reached the lake of open water that they had been heading for all day.

At 3:30 A.M., in fog and darkness, the *Florizel* and *Bonaventure*, also working close together in heavy ice, collided. The *Bonaventure*'s port anchor struck the *Florizel*'s starboard quarter, smashing her top plate below the mooring chock.

Bad luck for Joe Kean.

But the south-west wind had eased the ice off the land, and the ships, poking cautiously through the morning fog on the eighteenth, finally broke out into open water somewhere north of White Bay, and started steaming hell-for-leather towards St. Anthony, whose wireless station would give information on the seals as soon as they were in range.

A heavy downpour dispersed the fog and a westerly wind did the rest. By 11 A.M. it was fine and clear. At 12:15 they heard from St. Anthony: A string of seals sixty miles long had passed south-east the day before, just a few miles off the land. They could plot their position accurately within three or four miles. The seals were south of the ships by now.

Back along the coast they raced and headed out into the ice-field just south of the Grey Islands. They found that heavy Arctic ice, rafted and pinnacled, had been thrust up into a great series of pressure ridges. It was the heaviest, roughest ice that they had seen in years, and it was not until late afternoon that they sighted the seals.

But there it was! True whelping ice! Thousands, tens of thousands, of mother harps, moving among their whitecoats, which bawled and cried almost like human babies.

They forced their way close to them, put the men over the side on to the ice, and the killing began.

# CHAPTER FOUR

The men went over the sides by watches, each in charge of a master watch. They carried gaffs and sculping knives, honed to a razor-edge during the long hours of inactivity of the past few days. They carried tow ropes and lunch bags, with hard tack, oatmeal and raisins, for they might be long on the ice. Some of them also had small canteens, made from tin cans, belted to their waists; the canteens contained a potent mixture of molasses and Radway's Ready Relief, a patent medicine consisting mostly of alcohol. (The Old Man had no objection to alcohol used in medicines—that was what God had made it for—it was only as a *beverage* that it was forbidden.)

The men carried tall poles and flags—the heaviest things they had to handle—and a great nuisance, but necessary to mark the seals that belonged to each ship. The pelts would be collected together on ice pans big enough to keep them safe, and a flag stuck on each pan to mark ownership. The flags had distinctive colours and were also numbered. Each ship's flags could be told at a considerable distance.

But if the owner was out of sight, it was a simple matter to switch flags. Piracy was almost a recognized part of the game. No one questioned, later, where the pelts had come from. The winner was the skipper who got home with the most. The Old Man had no religious objection to that, either.

The watches were divided, in turn, into ice parties, each party in charge of an experienced sealer known as an ice master, who, unlike the master watch, had no authority on board ship, only on the ice. Each ice party worked as a unit, and its men were not supposed to separate.

They would approach a patch of seals and walk among them, clubbing the crying whitecoats. They cried real tears from big, appealing eyes, and the young men often found it very hard to kill them, at first. Only the fear of being labelled a "sissy" forced many a youngster to dispatch his first seal. Fortunately, the baby animals died quickly and easily. It took only a light blow on the nose or skull to end their lives. As the sealers flipped them over to begin sculping off the white pelts with their layers of subcutaneous fat, the limbs of the animals might still be jerking, spasmodically, but it was the reflex action of an animal already dead, like a chicken that runs with its head cut off.

Steam rose thickly from the fresh, warm carcasses. Blood flowed everywhere until the ice was crimson with it. And since skilled men could kill and sculp a whitecoat in three or four minutes, it did not take long to "clean up" a patch of seals. One fore flipper, including the leg and and shoulder meat, was left attached to the pelt, to be removed later as the pelts were stored on board ship. These heavily muscled shoulders were the "flippers" that Newfoundlanders regarded—and still regard—as one of the world's great delicacies. All the rest of the meat was left on the ice. Gulls would eat some of it, but most of it would finally sink into the sea when the ice melted far off to the south, and the sharks would gather to the refrigerated feast.

The gulls were here already, waiting. Among them hovered the pure white, pigeon-sized birds that the sealers called ice partridges. Ivory gulls from the Polar Pack, the world's most northerly sea birds, they were almost never seen on shore.

It was filthy work. Each man was soon coated with grease and blood. But he got used to it. Later the grease would turn rancid and stink abominably, but by that time the sealers' noses would be unable to smell it. The stinking fat commanded fancy prices in the markets, where it was turned into margarine, soap, lipstick, and other high-priced products with an oil base.

Exhausted, the men struggled back to their ships, towing "yaffles" of pelts on ropes. Where possible, the ship worked her way from pan to pan, and the piles of pelts were hoisted aboard with tackle rigged from the masts. It was slippery, unstable cargo, and was stowed in wooden pounds in the holds to keep it from shifting too much. If the holds were filled, additional pounds were built on deck. Every ship carried lumber for that purpose, as well as for making "side sticks"—the sort of primitive ladders that sealers used when going up and down over the sides.

Once pelts started coming on board, the captains abandoned all attempts to keep their ships clean. It would have been futile. Blood and grease coated the decks, and grew thicker by the day. Blood and grease was everywhere—the awful mixture even got into the drinking water in the casks until it was a brown, opaque liquid with a thick scum floating on it. Occasionally a ship's water supply developed thick bacterial cultures that made the men sick. Dysentery was common. But they could usually collect snow from the ice pans and melt it into fairly clean water.

Coaker wrote in his log that night: *"The crying of a herd of whitecoats is something not easily forgotten. . . . It is a pitiable cry, and it seems hard to slaughter those innocents. They are so purely white in appearance and so harmless.*

*"They realize their danger. The old ones race about the ice in all directions, tossing their heads erect, splurging into their blowing holes, then with a splurge they throw themselves again on the ice and rush towards the crying babies. Some of them stand by their young and lose their lives in protecting their babes who are constantly crying to their mothers."*

The rough, hummocky ice made killing difficult, and each ship averaged only five-hundred pelts that first evening.

Next day the kill began at dawn, and in earnest. By noon the *Nascopie* had cleaned up all the seals in her vicinity, picked up pelts and sealers, and steamed off looking for a new patch. In early afternoon Captain George Barbour sighted such a patch—a small one—and ordered a single watch to go after it. He also ordered a ship's boat and a bundle of torches to be placed on the ice near the men, in case he should be late returning for them. Then he steamed off in search of more seals. He did not know that William Coaker was among the sixty or so men whom he had left on the ice.

The wind was rising, and the sealers went quickly about their work, dispatching and sculping the small patch in about two hours. Coaker, in spite of his private feelings in the matter, was anxious to kill seals like a real man. He slaughtered and sculped nine whitecoats that day, bracing himself each time to kill the crying pups. Finally, they hauled all the pelts back to the boat, and piled them there, waiting for the *Nascopie*'s return. The ship was nowhere in sight.

"Cap'n Barbour put out tarches, sir," an old hand told Coaker. "That manes 'e'll be late gettin' back fer we. Ye can reckon on nine or ten o'clock I 'low."

Fog closed around them, and they lit a fire, cutting flagpoles into shavings with their sculping knives, then adding a little seal fat until it was blazing brightly. More flapoles were added until they had a cheerful fire. Then they sat around, swapping yarns, telling of their experiences at the ice. Several of the older men had survived the *Greenland* disaster of 1898, and Coaker listened to them eagerly, promising himself a long entry in his log that night:

"It were a good year fer swiles, sir. There we was, smack in the middle of fifty, sixty t'ousand of 'em, an only four ships. Cap'n Garge had the *Greenland* that year. Abe Kean were in the *Aurora*. Cap'n Darius Blandford had the *Iceland*, and Cap'n Alpheus Barbour were in the *Diana*."

"It were civil weather, too, ye mind," another old-timer put in. "We were killin' swiles from dawn to dark."

"Aye, it were. Fer six days we killed an' panned swiles, till we had enough to load the *Greenland* on deck an' below. But when we go to pick 'em up, I tell ye sir, they was gone—*stole!*"

We knowed who took 'em, too," the other old-timer growled. "It were Old Man Kean, that's who. Loaded 'e's ship with our pelts 'e did."

There were murmurs and grunts all round.

"On the seventeenth it were, nearly all our flags were out, an' we had twenty t'ousand swiles on pans, when we saw the *Aurora*'s men knock down a heap of our flags and stick up their own instead. Next day, damned if they didn't come up to another pan of ours and try to claim it fer theirs."

"Drawed their knives an' threatened to kill us, they did," the other interjected indignantly.

"They didn't get that pan, I can tell 'ee, but our cap'n went on board the *Aurora* an' spoke to Old Man Kean about stealin' our pans, an' ye know what 'e said? He had the face to say 'e didn't know what 'e's crew were doin' on the ice an' wouldn' hold 'e's self responsible."

Again there were angry mutterings.

"Anyway," the narrator continued, "we had to make up fer what were stole, tho' be rights we should o' been doin' nought but pick up pans be that time. So on Monday—that were March the twenty-first I 'low—Cap'n Barbour put out a watch an' took the rest o' we off three or four mile to the nor'east.

"Well, sir, he left, steamin' back t'ward the first watch, pickin' up pans o' swiles, but the starm come on, an' the *Greenland* never got back. It come a wonderful starm o' wind an' frost, sir, the like ye never see, an' in spite o' the ice shelters an' the fires, a lot o' men died. Some got weak in the mind, an' walked off an' never come back.

"Our crowd were doin' pretty well, mind ye; only one o' the men in our shelter died during' the night, an' a few others was gettin' low-minded, but Sam Burry come rushin' t'ward us, hollerin' that the *Greenland* were comin', an' we all left the shelter to walk to 'er . . . only we found out Sam were seein' the ship in 'e's head. It were too much fer some of our crowd, sir, an' they went foolish, too; some walked off into the starm, an' some walked into the sea. I don't mind much o' what happened after that, but I were picked up that marnin'. Others was out all the next night, and they was all froze, all but six or seven that were picked up next day, frost-burned somethin' cruel an' their minds gone wanderin' . . ."

"Twenty-three of 'em was never found, sir . . . never found," a sealer remembered.

"Cap'n Barbour had twenty-five carpses, froze junk-stiff on the for'ard hatch," another recalled, "but 'e didn't want to fersake the voyage, so long as the sick men got no worse. So 'e spent two days lookin' fer survivors, an' then planned to get back to the swilin', but some o' the men were still iceblind, an' their minds wanderin', so he give up the voyage an' headed fer home.

"It were a shockin' night even on board the *Greenland*," a man from another watch recalled. "There was pressure ridges twenty feet high, I 'low, with open water two mile wide t'other side. We was ordered to get out skiffs to go look fer the lost party, but the starm laid the ship over with her beam ends on the ice, an' here comes the coal and the provisions and the pelts rumblin' down into the scuppers an' holdin' 'er there. A wonder to God it were, sir, that she warn't lost, an' we workin' all night like dogs to save 'er an' get 'er right side up again."

It was the first time Coaker had heard the story first hand, and he stored it away for future use. No one could be blamed, perhaps, for the *Greenland* disaster. Old Man Kean, who had taken abuse because of it at the time, had been eight miles away, and didn't even know it had happened. Still, if he had instructed his men to respect the property of others, instead of stealing the *Greenland*'s pelts . . . if *all* sealing captains could rise above the pirating of rival's catches. . . .

The wind was now blowing almost a gale, and there was sleet in the air. The younger men played tag to keep warm, and Jim Harris of Harbour Grace did a dance while singing a ditty to the cheers of all hands. Earlier than expected, the *Nascopie* hove in sight, breaking ice towards them at full speed. Just after nightfall they scrambled thankfully up the side sticks and went to their suppers.

Captain Barbour had learned late that afternoon that Coaker was on the ice, and wasted no time getting back for them. Snow and rain, with winds of thirty-five miles per hour, now swept the ice-field, and Coaker was thankful to be back on board.

That night on the *Bonaventure* a sealer observed to his bunkmate, "Me boots is wore pretty thin." He held one up to the light.

His bunkmate, Henry Pridham of Petty Harbour, was a family man who knew all about repairing boots.

"I've some leather ye can have," he told his friend, rummaging in his kit bag, and handing the leather to him. Then he went up on deck for a look at the weather before turning in.

Blood, grease, sleet, and snow had mixed together on the *Bonaventure*'s deck, and no sooner did he step on it than Henry Pridham lost his footing. With a scream he plunged headlong into the hold among the men twenty feet below. His forehead struck the edge of a coal tub, which inflicted a deep wound. His screams when they moved him warned his mates that his back might be broken.

Return to port with the injured man? Unthinkable. The "doctor" (who was just a man in charge of the medicine chest, usually without any medical training) bandaged his head and put him in a bunk, where he passed into unconsciousness. Three days later, without ever opening his eyes, he died. He left a wife and four children. He was the first casualty at the seal hunt that year.

By Friday, March 20, all ships except the *Kite*, *Diana* and *Newfoundland* were into the seals. The *Kite* had taken Robert Peary on his first voyage in search of the North Pole, but she could not cope with *this* ice-field. But the ice-breakers were right in the thick of the fat. That day the *Beothic* killed five thousand, the *Stephano* six thousand. Next day the Old Man reported from the *Stephano* to Bowring's that he had ten thousand whitecoat pelts on board and four thousand on pans.

A hundred men from the *Beothic* failed to find their ship that night, for it was blowing half a gale, and thick with snow flurries, but Joe Kean, in the *Florizel*, found them and took them on board. Twelve of the *Florizel*'s own men were also astray, and after some hours of darkness gave up hope of finding any ship. They built an ice shelter, and kept a fire of seal pelts going. The pelts were "worth" $2.08 each, according to the arbitrary price announced by the merchants that year, but no matter what they were worth, they had to be sacrificed when there was danger of freezing to death. An hour before midnight, however, the *Beothic* found the lost party, and they clambered thankfully aboard.

All the seals now seemed to be "cleaned up," but on Monday, March 23, the *Stephano* found a fair-sized patch. The crew killed and panned four thousand, but much to the Old Man's disgust the ice opened up, and most of the panned seals floated away and were lost. By Tuesday there seemed to be no seals anywhere, and all ships were searching for new patches. Captain Abram Kean was in a bad mood that day. The upstart Billy Winsor in the *Beothic* was leading him by two thousand pelts, and threatened to be "highliner" for the year. Some of those two thousand might even be pans he had lost himself when the ice opened. It was a bitter thought.

They hunted seals all week with little result, everyone keeping Old Abe Kean in sight, believing that, sooner or later, he would find the Main Patch. By Friday, March 27, he still had not found it, and the ships were killing only scattered seals.

The much smaller fleet to the west in the Gulf was doing well, with an estimated seventy thousand pelts on board—not a bad voyage, even if it ended right then. The owners estimated that same day that the ships at The Front had 130,000 pelts on board. But the seals had vanished. And no one had seen the *Newfoundland*.

Where was the Main Patch?

And where was the missing ship?

# CHAPTER FIVE

The *Newfoundland* had done nothing, and her captain was desperate. The old ship had let him down. She had squatted in the ice of Notre Dame Bay, and had stayed there, her holds still empty apart from the few hundred seals they had taken more than a week before. With stack smoking and engines laboring she had inched her way to nowhere.

"We'm jinked," the men muttered among themselves blaming the two stowaways who were thought to be "jinkers."

"Should've put 'em ashore," others growled, casting black glances at the two youngsters breaking their backs working with the firemen, stoking the insatiable furnace.

But the men did not growl too loudly. Wes Kean had made good sealing voyages before now; he was a go-getter, like his old man, and if the food was plain, at least it wasn't scarce.

There were days when they worked like dogs trying to free the *Newfoundland*, days when she shuddered and complained with the effort to move forward. They laboured in gangs with steel-tipped stabber poles to ease the rafted ice that piled up against her sides, to break a path, even a little way ahead, pushing, sweating, straining, and cursing the ice (but mildly, for it was bad luck to curse the elements). When it was so tight as to threaten to crush her, they got out the dynamite, packed in cans with waterproof percussion caps. They fused it and pushed it under the ice with the poles. Then, as they set it off, the ice rose with a roar, buckled, cracked, splintered, a geyser of fragments shooting skywards, men ducking as dangerous chunks hailed down on them, then grabbing the stabber poles to make the best of the cracks that had opened up. Labouring mightily, their ship crashed through the floes, butting them with her scarred bow, her oaken timbers yielding but never cracking, until she was brought to a halt again by the unyielding floe.

Some days she laboured two or three miles, some days less, barely enough to offset the southward drift of the ice. And yet the seals were getting nearer, for the fleet and the seals were drifting south with the ice.

Wes spent much of his time in the chilly lookout barrel on the ship's mast, eye glued to a spy-glass. The smoke on the northern horizon was tantalizing.

"They're killing swiles up there, George, I'm sure of it," he would agonize to Second Hand Tuff.

They worked the *Newfoundland* northward, pitting their puny strength against the pressures of the ice-field, levering the pans aside, hauling on hawsers to help drag the ship through tight "leads" as their fathers had done in the days of sail.

"This 'minds me o' the story me grandfather told about the *Lovely Lass*," grunted one exhausted sealer from Conception Bay, "the year her crew walked all the way from Baccalieu to The Funks, towin' her."

"I heerd tell o' that story," another rejoined. "How far would it be, do ye reckon?"

"Hundred mile or thereabouts, I 'low. I never give no heed to that ol' yarn before, but now I half believes 'tis true."

They pushed, strained, and worked like galley slaves, as eager as their captain to get into the fat. They were out there to earn their thirty or forty or fifty dollars—even more, perhaps, if they had exceptional luck.

Wes grew more desperate daily. The season for whitecoats was a short one. Three weeks, at most, separated the start of the hunt from the time when the young seals began to head for the water. Once in the sea they would start swimming for the Arctic, beyond the outer edge of the ice-field, and then you could kiss good-bye to all hopes of a paying voyage. You could still hunt old seals, using guns, but most of them would escape into the water, wounded, and finally sink. Old Man Kean reckoned that for every old seal brought to shore, twenty others had been sunk. He was opposed to such destructive hunting, and anyway, as the sealers said, "There was no money in old fat." Wes could see his reputation as a "jowler," a successful skipper, going swiftly down the drain if he drew a blank while other ships got a load. His mood grew black, and the crew trod softly.

For the crew it wasn't so hard. They were usually busy at the bunkers or working to free the ship, and at night they settled down to story-telling, to singing, to dancing to a small accordion or mouth organ, and to swapping eerie tales of the supernatural. Occasionally, under cover of darkness, the teenagers, as full of mischief at sea as they were at home, would sneak up the rigging to the side of fresh beef for the officers' dinners that hung there, and hack off enough to flavour a pot of soup. In high spirits the stolen luxury would be cooked on one of the "bogeys" in the hold.

There was the usual grumbling about food. One Sunday they had canned salt beef, but that was exceptional. Each Friday they were given raw salt fish, which they could boil or roast themselves. But most of the time it was hard tack and tea, with raw salted fatback instead of butter. They drank hundreds of gallons of tea, ate barrels of raw fat pork and numberless bags of hard tack, and got more sleep than they needed.

By March 26, there was just a "sign" of seals. Scouting groups brought in fifteen pelts that day.

"We're getting handy to the swiles," Wes fretted. "They're close by. Damn! If we could only get moving!"

The barometer was exceptionally high: 30.60. Charles Green, the navigator, decided that little could be foretold from that. Now if only the *Newfoundland* had been equipped with a deck thermometer that showed if the temperature was rising or falling, he might be able to make an accurate guess at the weather. A rising "glass" with rising temperature meant fine weather, almost for sure. A rising glass with falling temperature was more likely to portend a gale from the northwest, maybe with snow flurries, and almost certainly with hard frost; the opposite of fine weather. Without a deck thermometer there was no way of telling which way the weather was going. They spent another profitless night wedged in the ice-field, but next day a heavy swell (evidence of a storm somewhere in the Atlantic) began to roll beneath the ice-field, loosening it enough to let the *Newfoundland* work northward. Soon they found themselves in a small, scattered patch of whitecoats.

"Get 'em!" Wes ordered.

In a few minutes they had killed and sculped about twenty seals.

"Stow 'em down."

The pelts, dripping blood and fat, were winched aboard, and the ship pushed forward again. But she was creeping northward so slowly that the captain's patience could stand it no longer.

"The swiles are out there. Go get 'em!" he ordered. The four watches were ready and waiting. Heading north-west, they soon outdistanced the ship and vanished among peaks and pinnacles of rough ice. Before nightfall they returned, exhausted from the hard slogging in the rough ice, towing behind them a total of three hundred pelts. They were, indeed, getting close.

Although Wes didn't know it, no ship at The Front, just then, was taking pelts. After the first big kill the seals had eluded them while they drifted south-east with the ice-field, criss-crossing the floes in quest of the herd. Billy Winsor had stowed down twenty-four thousand pelts on the *Beothic*, Abraham Kean eighteen thousand on the *Stephano*, Joe Kean fourteen thousand on the *Florizel*. They needed almost twice that number for a "bumper trip."

The smaller ships in the Gulf were well-nigh loaded. The *Southern Cross*, credited with about twenty thousand, was already heading for Cabot Strait and the trip home along Newfoundland's south coast.

On this day, far away to the south-west, a killer storm was spawned.

An enormous high pressure area, centred near Bermuda, its mass of dry, heavy air pressing down over half the western Atlantic, was feeding winds in a vast anti-clockwise motion into the Gulf of Mexico, from which warm, humid air was sweeping northward into the central states. This warm, moist air made a vast circle about a second high that was pushing cold, dry air outwards over the province of Manitoba and into the United States. A deep low was developing between the two systems, a whirlpool of warm, moist air, slowly contracting upon itself, drawing hundreds of cubic miles of air, and water enough to deluge half a continent, into a slowly rotating funnel, rising and spreading, and forming circular cloud masses far above the continental heartland.

Rain was already falling over Mississippi, dense downpours over the corn belt, and the first showers of the coming storm were bringing rain and snow to the Great Lakes and southern Ontario.

Another deep low, off the Labrador coast, 450 miles north-west of The Funks, was sending another eruption of moist air into the stratosphere, sucking winds in from the ocean to replace the rising air mass, and kicking up the storm that was causing the swell beneath the ice-field. Even as far south as Notre Dame Bay the edges of this storm brought bad weather. The *Florizel* reported to Bowring's: "Weather poor; snowing all day . . . cannot see any other ship."

And all the while the storm over the central states was pressing eastward . . .

That night the *Newfoundland* steamed westward, making slow progress through heavy ice. Wes Kean was aiming for the smoother sheet ice that he had seen to the westward from his topmast barrel, and where he thought the Main Patch of seals should lie. It was not certain that he could reach the sheet ice, however, for heavy Arctic ice, pressed up into hummocks and pressure ridges, had invaded the slob and pan ice where he was now working, making the ice-field both difficult and dangerous to a ship like the *Newfoundland*.

Saturday found her deep into the Arctic ice, making little headway, and Wes Kean spoke despairingly to George Tuff: "The swiles are handy, George, I *know* it. That looks to me like whelping ice, off there to the west'ard."

At 10 A.M. he could stand it no longer. Leaving the ship to Tuff, he took three men, went over the side and struck off to the west, his long sealskin coat flapping around his ankles. By noon a fresh breeze was blowing and there was some snow. Labouring mightily, the *Newfoundland* tried to follow her captain. All on board kept an anxious eye open for him and his three men as the wind increased and the snow thickened. It was nearly four o'clock when they appeared out of the flurries and climbed on board. They had not found the seals, or reached the sheet ice where Wes believed them to be. By seven o'clock the wind was howling through the rigging and thick snow isolated them from the world. The ice moved under the swell, but still held them fast, and the murmurs rose again, "We'm jinked." Where was the Kean luck now?

March 28 was a grim anniversary. On this day sixteen years before, the S.S. *Greenland* had sailed into St. John's harbour with her flag at half mast, "a floating chamber of horrors" with the twenty-five frozen corpses on deck and twenty-three men missing. They had died at just about the same place where the *Newfoundland* was now trapped.

Everyone had heard, too, that in the home of one of the victims at the time of the storm a ten-year-old lad was on his way to bed when his big brother, who was at the ice, stopped him on the stairs and pleaded, "Harry, give me a lend of your cap." The apparition vanished a moment later, but the family was certain some accident had happened at the ice-field, and that their son was dead.

The sea each year must claim its share of victims, the men in the hold assured each other. It wailed and shrieked in its demand for human life. They were firm believers in fate. When a man was marked for death nothing could save him. This belief helped to support them in danger, for its corollary was "Ye'll not die, me son, till yer time is come."

At some places along the coast evil spirits lurked, showing false lights and luring ships to destruction. These were the Jack-o-lanterns, and wise men turned their eyes away from them. Sometimes, though, the Jack-o-lantern, determined to seize a victim, would give chase, and woe betide the man who could not outstrip the light. Those wise to the ways of the Jack-o-lantern carried a horn-handled knife. When the light approached, they would stick it in the ground and set fire to the handle, then run for their lives. The Jack-o-lantern could not pass until the horn had all burned off.

And who could laugh in the face of the banshee, the "auld witch" that keened on the wind in the face of approaching death? And didn't the souls of friends and relatives, gone before, tap and scratch at doors where death would soon liberate one whose end was near? If you listened, you could easily fancy the banshee wailing in the *Newfoundland*'s rigging tonight.

But the denizens of the "world between" might be good as well as evil. How else could you explain the lights often seen on shoals where no light was set? Some time in the past a ship had struck that very shoal, and gone down with all hands. Now the spirits saw that a light was set at the onset of a storm to warn fellow sailors of the danger.

One of the older sealers from the north told about Mrs. John Dower of Conche in White Bay, whose love for her sealer husband had caused her great anguish whenever he went to the ice. On March 10, forty-one years before, the vessel *Eleanor*, owned and commanded by John Dower, had left Conche for the seal hunt. About a week later Mrs. Dower complained of feeling ill. Her condition worsened rapidly, and within six hours she was dead.

The news spread, and the neighbours gathered, but as she lay "waking," friends from far and near remarked that poor Mrs. Dower looked as if she were merely sleeping. Then, on the third day of the wake, word was passed that the *Eleanor* was coming into harbour with her flag at half mast. This could mean only that somebody had died on board ship, for in those days there was no communication between ship and shore, and Captain Dower could not possibly know that his wife was dead.

Then a strange thing happened. From Mrs. Dower's body came a long, weary sigh, and the cold, waxen figure began to move. Before the terror-stricken eyes of the good people, colour and warmth returned to her cheeks, and she sat up, murmuring, "I am tired . . . I have been far . . . I have been with John."

It was true, they said. John Dower later told how his wife had come over the ice to him. He had seen her coming and, believing her to be dead, had lowered his flag and sailed for home, his heart full of grief. When he saw his wife alive and well his joy was unbounded. He never went to the ice again, but it was always his proud boast that his good wife had gone and returned from the ice-field even quicker than his smart little ship.

The young men on board loved to hear the old tales, and to frighten themselves so much that they wouldn't venture on deck alone at night. But some of the old hands disliked this talk of death and "signs." Such talk was bad luck, they said, like black cats and stowaways, and sailing on a Friday.

*That*, perhaps along with the stowaways, was what had "jinked" the *Newfoundland* this trip, for though she had cleared from Wesleyville on Thursday, it was really Friday before she got away from Flowers Island—and *Friday the thirteenth*, at that, the unluckiest day in the calendar. They wondered at the nerve of Old Man Kean who had chosen to lead the fleet of ice-breakers out through The Narrows at St. John's on such a date. This was sure to be a "hoodooed" voyage.

If the evil spirits had their eyes on the ice-field, they were working with powerful allies.

Both the Bermuda high and the Manitoba high had drifted eastward. Now between the two huge centres of high pressure there was a long funnel, or trough, pointing north-eastward towards Newfoundland. This was the only way that the storm centre could go. And the disturbance was now deepening, fed by the continual flow of moist air from the south.

Meanwhile, the Labrador low had moved off into the Atlantic, bringing strong north-west winds and flurries to the ice-fields, and leaving a clear path for the sub-tropical cyclone, not only north-eastward to the Grand Banks and Newfoundland, but on the ice-fields of The Front. A witches' brew of wind and snow was coming to the boil.

# CHAPTER SIX

On Sunday it was still blowing a gale from the north and the *Newfoundland* was jammed, with only four hundred pelts in her hold, and only two or three days left before the whitecoats began taking to the water. Wes Kean already felt a sense of disgrace. His men watched him pace the bridge, and their mood matched his.

"We could've got more swiles huntin' from shore," they complained. But they felt better after their Sunday service, with lusty hymn-singing in the hold. Those on watch shivered as the wind sang a different tune through the rigging and the rafted ice groaned and creaked against the ship's sides.

No seals were sighted by any ship at The Front that day. Captain Winsor reported to his owners that the *Beothic* had twenty-five thousand pelts stowed down, and would return to port about April 1, undoubtedly highliner of the fleet.

At 7 P.M. a wireless message from Channel on the south-west corner of Newfoundland informed St. John's that the *Southern Cross* had passed there at 6:30, about seven miles off, with all flags flying. This meant she was loaded and heading for home. She should reach port late Tuesday night, or early Wednesday morning.

By Monday, March 30, the fleet of steel ice-breakers had drifted south-east with the ice-field until they had passed The Funks, more than 150 miles from the place they had originally found the seals. The seals, of course, would have drifted with them and were assumed to be somewhere close by, though they still had not been found. The big ships were only "picking up scattered seals," which meant that they might increase their catch by a hundred or a few hundred in a day, not by several thousand, as they would if they were "in the fat."

The weather was clear with moderate winds, and the fleet was scouting the edges of the heavy Arctic ice-field, with its rafters and pinnacles and pressure ridges. A heavy swell running through the pack had permitted the *Newfoundland* to work her way northward, though she was still in heavy ice that yielded grudgingly to the swell.

Then at last, at eight o'clock in the morning, with the sun at his back, Wes Kean sighted the ships skippered by his father and his brother. The *Stephano* and *Florizel* were far away, but unmistakable. He was excited—almost elated. Perhaps, after all, there was still time to retrieve his lost fortunes. At last he felt that he was part of the sealing fleet. His ship was making tortuous progress through the ice, but at least he was moving.

The *Stephano* was stopped, temporarily, with steering gear trouble, and Abram Kean was able to direct his full attention to the *Newfoundland*, which he now sighted for the first time in more than two weeks. Had she found the seals? He radioed to Joe, in the *Florizel*, to go on board the *Newfoundland* if he got the chance, and find out how Wes had fared with the hunt. Joe did not need to board his brother's ship. He manoeuvred his powerful ice-breaker alongside, and they conferred by shouting from the bridge to bridge.

Wes told Joe of his belief that the seals lay to the west on the sheet ice, and of his ill luck so far. Then, with a commiserative wave of the hand, the older brother moved off towards the *Stephano*, and promptly relayed the information to the Old Man.

Navigator Charles Green noted at noon that the barometer was again very high, and jotted it down: 30.60. Again he wished he had a deck thermometer, and cursed the stinginess of the owners in not providing one. Abnormally high readings needed almost as much watching as abnormally low ones. The last high reading had been the forerunner of Saturday's gale. Perhaps they were due for more of the same.

All around him, Wes noted, ships were appearing—chasing after the Old Man, he well knew, though maintaining a discreet distance.

In his log, William Coaker noted, *"Every captain closely watches the movements and actions of Captain Abram Kean. I don't believe any captain is content when he is not in a position to know or judge what Captain Abram is doing. I state this not because I have any kindly feelings towards Captain Abram, but because I wish to give all concerned in this narrative their proper due."*

Of the Old Man's closest rival he wrote: *"Captain William Winsor is a pushing young man and will, if he lives, become one of the foremost and most successful of our sealing masters. He has plenty of push and his judgement of seals is sound, his one fault being a careless disregard of his men when taking seals and his devil-daring in cutting off other crews. He came close to cutting down a pan of ice containing some of our crew while pelting seals. Some of our men had to leave off pelting and run."*

Of the captain of the *Nascopie* he wrote: *"George Barbour is a very steady customer, always cool and collected and very careful over his men. They all respect him."*

That morning from St. Pierre off Newfoundland's south coast a wireless operator reported: "Three-masted black-painted steamer with a yellow funnel going south-east just passing now." The ship could only be the *Southern Cross*. The *Eric* would have called at Channel to land part of her crew. The *Viking* and *Terra Nova* had white funnels with Bowring's red insignia. So Baine Johnston's *Southern Cross* would be the first sealer into port that year—or so everyone believed. But the gods of the storm had other plans.

The hunt now concentrated around the edge of the Arctic ice. The steel ships fought to penetrate the jungle of boulders and ridges that extended north-north-west and south-south-east, a massive obstruction that was bent outwards at the centre like the bulge of a bow, pressing westward into the smoother ice. The *Newfoundland* was working towards the sheet ice a few miles south-east of the bulge. The *Stephano*, her steering gear repaired, was also working westward, but in the vicinity of the bulge itself.

Approaching the edge of the heavy ice in late afternoon, Abram Kean came upon some scattered seals and ordered three men over the side to get them. They were towing the pelts back to the *Stephano*, and one sealer was approaching the stern, when the Old Man, spying to the west from the barrel, spotted a thick patch of seals on the low sheet ice almost directly ahead.

"Swiles!" he rumbled, and descended from the barrel, barely able to conceal the excitement he felt. He shouted to a deck hand, waving towards the sealers on the ice: "Throw 'em a flag, me son."

The deck hand hastily threw a crimson flag overboard, and the Old Man, leaning over the rail, yelled, "Flag yer seals, me son, we're headin' west'ard. Wait till the other fellers comes up; tell 'em to slip their seals with yours on that pan, then all of ye come on through the ice after us—we'll be over on the small ice ahead."

The man obediently slipped his tow of seals, planted the flag, and stood waiting for the others while the *Stephano* ground her way towards the sheet ice and Old Man's delighted blue eyes beheld one of the loveliest sights he had ever seen: For there on the smooth ice ahead was the Main Patch he had so diligently sought for more than a week. They lay in a string at least half a mile wide, extending for miles to the north-north-west on his starboard bow, and to the south-south-east on his port. The ice was alive with them!

Wes Kean had been right all the time. The Main Patch was on the sheet ice west of the Arctic floes. Had he been in charge of one of the ice-breakers, he might well have been the high-liner of the fleet that year. As it was, he had shown the Old Man, through Joe, where to get the swiles.

Captain Kean lost no time. "Over the side an' at 'em, me sons!" he roared in high glee.

Perhaps he felt some gratitude towards Wes, who had guessed correctly where the seals would be found. In any case, he remembered their bargain.

Hist the after-derrick," he shouted to a deck hand, then gave his full attention to the seals.

The *Stephano* steamed north-west, around the bulge of heavy ice, dropping men as she went. In turn, the men left a bloody trail of dead seals and panned pelts piled beneath her crimson flags. They had killed about fifteen hundred before the Old Man brought them on board for the night to grab a few hours' rest.

The *Florizel*, in spite of Wes Kean's advice, had been steaming north-east until a wireless message from the *Stephano* ordered her to turn about. Joe Kean steamed westward until he came to the seals that had spilled over from the Main Patch into the rough ice. Then he set his men to killing.

Captain John Parsons of the *Bonaventure* had been working his ship eastward, not far from the *Florizel*. Seeing the latter turn about he put two and two together, and began to chase Joe Kean westward. But the ice was so heavy that darkness had fallen before he arrived at the patch Joe Kean was working. Then he happily burned down for the night with the sound of bawling whitecoats in his ears.

The *Stephano* had burned down about two miles north-west of the bulge, her pelts waiting to be picked up at day-break. The *Newfoundland* was three or four miles south-south-east of the bulge, and firmly jammed.

It was a calm night where the sealers lay, but Captain George Barbour, a veteran who knew all the signs of weather, noted "mares' tails" in the sky and saw that the sun was shimmering as if it had been dipped in a bowl of crystal. "The sun is showing for a storm," he said soberly to his second hand. The barometer was still unusually high, but he knew that rain or snow, probably with high winds, might be expected.

The storm centre had now contracted to its smallest diameter, with violence concentrated around its heart. It had developed tremendous energy as it began prowling across the southern edge of the Banks. The *Southern Cross* was steering directly into its path.

Wes Kean ate a gloomy supper. He had seen the signal that he alone understood on the Old Man's ship—the hoisted derrick that meant "swiles." They were exactly where he had predicted for many days past that they would be, but being right gave him little comfort. They were too far away for the *Newfoundland*'s crew to work, and she had come to a dead stop once again. The ice ahead was even thicker and rougher. The chance of reaching the seals seemed small indeed.

The master watches ate silently. It was no time for chit-chat. Only Navigator Charles Green ventured an opinion about the weather, as he did almost every evening: "We have a high glass today; it might mean fine weather tomorrow."

Wes growled, "What do you know about it?"

The other officers were aware of Wes Kean's animosity towards Green, whose master's certificate the young captain envied. Green took the rebuffs smoothly. They were the price he paid for being an outsider.

After supper Wes retired to his cabin to think things over. He hadn't counted on getting jammed. In his four years as master he had dealt with more than one crisis. One year he had successfully put down a mutiny and returned with a bumper load. Another year he had completed a successful trip even though he had to deal with an outbreak of smallpox among the crew. What would the Old Man do, he wondered, in a jam like this?

He went topside, prowled the deck, looking at the lights of the steel fleet twinkling frostily on the horizon. Gazing at the lights he made a decision, and went below to the cabin. It was the most crucial decision in Wes Kean's life, but he did not make it hastily.

Master Watch Thomas Dawson was in the cabin alone, getting a mug-up before going on watch.

Father gave me the sign this evening that there's plenty of swiles over there just as I said."

"Yah! Looks like they're burned down in the fat, Cap'n."

"Tom, if we can't get ahead tonight, the b'ys will have to walk to the *Stephano* tomorrow."

Dawson nodded. It was no earth-shaking news. Many of them had walked greater distances over the sea ice in their time.

By now Wes had it figured out: "Father will tell you where to go when you get there. If there's a lot of swiles, you'll be killing all day and it'll be too far for you to come back. So two watches will go aboard the *Stephano* and two will go aboard the *Florizel* for the night. You'll be as well off on those two ships as you'd be aboard this one."

"Sounds all right, Cap'n." Dawson knew that Captain Abe Kean and Captain Joe Kean would accept the *Newfoundland*'s men without a murmur.

"That's what we'll do, then. Are ye on duty watch tonight?"

"Next watch is mine, Cap'n."

"If the ice slackens at all, and there's any chance of getting ahead, call me, Tom. I'm goin' to turn in, now. Be sure and call me if there's a chance to move." He went to his cabin to get what sleep he could, and later, when Dawson went on watch, he spread the word of tomorrow's hunt among his men. They were cheered at the prospect of getting into the fat.

Dawson called the captain once during the night. The ice had slackened just a little. They got up steam and forced the *Newfoundland* ahead, backing and butting. She made good a few times her own length through the ice-floes towards the barrier of rafters that lay ahead, then was jammed tight once more. Disappointed, Wes turned in to sleep until dawn.

# CHAPTER SEVEN

The sun rose in a blood-red sky. It was the last day of March, and the air was soft with spring. There was a light southerly breeze with a tendency to back to the east, bringing the barest hint of rawness. The barometer on the *Stephano* at 5 A.M. stood at 29.60.

The *Florizel, Bonaventure*, and *Stephano* already had men killing seals, and Frededrick Yetman, second hand to Captain Abram Kean, on duty in the barrel, noted that the *Newfoundland* was in the same place as yesterday, obviously jammed, five or six miles to the south-east. The *Florizel* and *Bonaventure* were to the east in the heavy ice, almost within gunshot of each other. Their men were working the same patches. Further south, beyond the *Newfoundland*, the *Bellaventure* was steaming through loose ice.

Whitecoats were bawling all around, and it was barely light when the *Stephano* began working north-west through the small ice as the Old Man dropped his men in patches of seals with an encouraging bellow, "Go on, me sons!" By 7 A.M., the last watch had been dropped, and the *Stephano* turned about, heading for the seals she had panned the day before.

As they steamed among their crimson flags to the west of the bulge of heavy ice, Yetman could see the flag they had left in the heavy ice the day before, bearing east-south-east a couple of miles. They were now much nearer to the *Newfoundland*, which lay about four miles away, he thought. She showed no signs of activity.

Having reached his most southerly pan, Captain Kean now turned the *Stephano* about and steamed slowly north-west picking up panned seals. It was at this time that they saw to the south-west, off her port beam, another patch of seals, a mile or two away—fourteen hundred to fifteen hundred the Old Man estimated, but since his crews were working to the northward, he decided to leave them until later.

Gradually, they worked to the north-west, stowing down their pelts. Yetman was sure they had not missed any pans and that all their flags were back on board, with the exception of the single flag left inside the edge of the heavy ice the day before, marking the single pan of pelts taken just before they had discovered the Main Patch. He was wrong. There was at least one other flag that they had missed, and it seems likely that there were two.

By 8 A.M. the barometer had fallen to 29.50.

Before sun-up Wes had been in the barrel scanning the horizon for the position of the other ships. The *Florizel* and *Bonaventure* were, he estimated, seven or eight miles northward; the *Stephano* was nearer—four or five miles; the *Bellaventure* was well to the south, heading northward through loose ice beyond the edge of the Arctic pack. *She* would have no trouble getting into the fat, he thought enviously.

It promised to be a soft morning, spring-like, but he had no time to admire the weather. The barometer outside his cabin was standing far above 30, and that was enough for him. Quickly, he reviewed his plan of the night before. He wondered about the younger master watches, how well they could be trusted at such a distance from the ship. Now if George Tuff were in charge of the hunt . . .

As second hand, Tuff was in charge of the ship's operation and did not have to go on the ice with the men. Wes had no right to ask him to do it. Tuff now had his eye glued to the spy-glass, trained on the ships to the north. The ice between them, he noted, was swarming with men, a sure sign that they were into a big patch of seals. He did not notice the disc of the sun rising above the glittering white rim of the ice-field behind him or the small patch of cloud gathered there.

As Wes took the glass from his second hand for another survey of the ice, he noted uncomfortably that the men were going to have rough going before they could reach the seals. He had never seen ice more ragged and rafted than that lying to the north-west of his ship. After half a mile or so they would be clambering over pressure ridges all the way. Still, they could do it, though it might slow them for an hour or two.

"It's hard to see the other ships right in the thick o' the swiles, and us not able to reach 'em, George," he said to the second hand.

"No trouble to walk to 'em, Cap'n," Tuff said. "I've walked farthern than that many a time."

"You mean you'd go, and lead the men?"

"Gladly, Cap'n."

"It's a good distance."

Tuff scoffed. "We've walked at least twice as far as that fer seals."

Wes breathed a sigh of relief. He had not asked Tuff to go. Tuff had volunteered.

"All right, George. You go down and lead the men."

Charles Green was in the cabin when Wes and Tuff entered. On deck the common hands were busy preparing for the hunt, coiling tow ropes over their shoulders, testing the edges of knives, filling sacks with hard tack, rolled oats and raisins. In the cabin Green listened as Wes and Tuff made their plans.

"Make straight fer the *Stephano*, George. From there ye'll be able to find out exactly where the seals are. Father will send ye to them. I can't give you any orders as to what ye'll do when ye get there. I'll leave it all with ye. Once ye're away from the ship ye'll have to work out yer own plans."

It was a grave responsibility, but Tuff accepted it lightly, and the three men went topside into the bustle and noise of the deck.

"In case ye get into the seals, and are panning for any length o' time, ye reckon on the *Stephano* for the night," Wes cautioned. This remark was heard by Green, but Tuff's attention was already with the men now going over the side, and apparently he did not hear the captain.

By 6 A.M. the sun was veiled, and to Captain Charles Green the sky looked threatening, in spite of the balmy air. The soft breeze was still blowing from the south, but he privately thought that it was not going to be a fine day for long.

A few old hands who knew the weather signs squinted at the hazy sun and noted with distaste twin reflections of yellowish light, like minor suns, one on either side. Stephen Jordan remarked on it. "Sun hounds," he said. "Never boded no good, sun hounds . . ." But most sealers thought the slight haze in the sky of no significance. They had more important things to think about.

John Howlett had been on duty all that night hauling coal out of the hold for the stokers. Now at 6 A.M. he was eating breakfast, listening to the bustle of men preparing for the hunt, and wondering whether he should join them. He soon made up his mind. He wanted seals as badly as anyone; he was young, and lack of sleep hardly bothered him; he would go. When he went on deck he, too, noted the sun hounds. By this time they had changed formation, looking rather like a skein of knotted wool, one knot on either side of the sun.

Some of the sealers, he noted, were removing heavy jackets and extra guernseys, and ducking below to tuck them into their bunks. Walking in this weather was going to be warm work and most of them were dressed for it in short jackets and woollen caps. A few more were taking bearings on the *Stephano* with cheap pocket compasses. Tuff, seeing to it that they carried enough ropes and flagpoles, was hustling them over the side. He himself did not have a compass, since his duties were supposed to be confined to the ship, but the four master watches were each supposed to carry one from the ship's stores. Master Watch Arthur Mouland discovered, too late, that he had left his compass on board ship. It was the first time in his life he had gone on the ice without one.

The wooden deck of the *Newfoundland* had begun to steam in the warmth of the sun when Wes Kean ordered them away from the ship at 7 A.M.

"Get ready to follow your master watch," he bellowed from the bridge. "The master watches will follow the second hand."

Tuff, complete with snow goggles (he had been ice-blind before), led off, and soon the bustle and confusion died away as the men fell in, one behind the other, for their winding trek across the floes.

From the bridge Wes Kean watched his men heading for the heavy ice, and let his gaze wander around the horizon to the *Bellaventure* working easily to the south. She was enveloped, he noted, in a kind of dancing heat haze, and suddenly he had second thoughts about the weather. He rushed down to consult the barometer, and it reassured him, registering "fair weather." The old glass had not been checked for years, but it had served him well, and he had no worries about its accuracy.

Green also checked the glass, then went to the cabin to write up the log. The glass had fallen by 20 tenths, he noted, since he had last logged it, at noon the day before. That did not necessarily mean any drastic change—milder weather, perhaps. Nevertheless, the early morning signs, in his estimation, had all the earmarks of a storm coming up. It might come slowly, of course—perhaps not until the seals were already panned.

At St. John's in the shop of Roper, the nautical optician, the barograph at 4 A.M. that day had registered 29.60. By 8 A.M. it was 29.50. Though the weather was still mild and hazy at St. John's, the outer fringes of the storm had already reached the south coast of Newfoundland, where an inch of snow had fallen, and the weather was closing in rapidly. It was the ice crystals, flying far ahead of this storm and far above it, that had created the sun hounds over the ice-field at dawn, refracting the sun's rays, and displacing false images of it to left and right.

Tuff was a careful man. He had never forgotten his experience in the *Greenland*, and had no intention of taking chances. Once into the rough ice, he charted his course by a compass passed to him by one of the master watches. He also ordered the men who had been working in the bunkers to take their mitts, blackened with coal dust, and use them to mark the ice pinnacles as they passed. The blackened peaks stood out like beacons, marking the trail, back to within half a mile of the ship.

Some of the young men, exhilarated at the prospect of action after all the days trapped in the ice-fields, climbed the pressure ridges, using their hooked gaffs like mountaineers' picks. The exertion made them sweat, and they paused to remove guernseys and bare their chests. It was so warm that some of them even stripped to the waist. But the wind, now blowing from the south-east, kept backing a little easterly, bringing a touch of rawness and making some of them uneasy.

"If the wind comes from the east, 'tis good for neither man nor beast," somebody quoted.

They laughed, and trudged on.

To Cecil Mouland, his cousin Ralph, their friends Bill and Dave Cuff, young Art Mouland, Phil and Dave Abbott, the excursion seemed wonderfully exciting. Through the grapevine they had learned that they were to stay that night on the *Stephano*, the newest and finest ice-breaker in the world. To lads from a little cove in Notre Dame Bay the prospect was almost overwhelming.

"She's a beauty, that one is," said Cecil, who had sailed on many a schooner, but never on anything like the *Stephano*.

Their master watch was Jacob Bungay, and they were in the middle of the long line of sealers snaking among the floes. Not far ahead in the line was Albert John Crewe and his father, Reuben. Not far behind came Edward Tippett with his three sons, Abel, Norman, and William.

There was little water to be seen among the floes, but plenty of snow, and their hobnailed boots beat a path in it. It was the roughest, toughest ice they had ever seen, and behind them, here and there along the path, heavy flagpoles had been surreptitiously dropped. They had a long way to go; the ice was rough, the air too warm to burden themselves unnecessarily. Their gaffs they kept, of course. No man would walk the length of himself over the ice without his gaff, but the flag-poles seemed like a lot of useless lumber.

The first to see the *Newfoundland*'s crew on the ice was Second Hand Nathan Kean of the *Florizel*. He spotted them at 8 A.M. and informed Captain Joe. Joe took one look, then turned back to his own crew, who were busy killing seals. The *Newfoundland*'s men were still some miles away.

Southward of the *Florizel* the *Stephano* eased along, her winches clattering as deck hands hauled seals aboard and stowed them away. Her decks were slippery with oil as the mild weather thawed pelts that had frozen the night before.

In the barrel, Second Hand Yetman was relieved by the Old Man and went down for breakfast. He took his time over tea and a smoke. His brother George was the officers' cook, and both enjoyed the privilege of being brothers-in-law to Abram Kean, their sister Caroline having been the Old Man's wife for more than forty years.

It was getting nearer 9 A.M. when Yetman returned to the barrel. Almost at once he spotted the men from the *Newfoundland* still far away and directly in line with their shp.

"The *Newfoundland*'s crew is on the ice, Skipper," he called to the Old Man. "It seems they'm headed this way."

The Old Man, more interested in picking up seals than in what other crews were doing, promptly made the mistake of assuming that the *Newfoundland*'s crew were just then leaving their ship, instead of having been on the ice for the past two hours. It was the first of many mistakes that he was to make that day.

"Ahl rate!" he called in his flat, Bonavista Bay dialect, and turned back to getting every possible bit of speed out of the crew that was stowing down. By now there were more panned seals than he was likely to pick up that day, and he was anxious to get them aboard. It was an hour later before he thought again of the *Newfoundland*'s men, and went to have a look from the barrel on the mast. They seemed to be headed for his ship, sure enough, but were still a fair distance south of the bulge in the heavy ice, while he was a fair distance north of it. For the first time, too, he noted the overcast (it had now thickened) and decided that rain and fog were coming—typical April weather. He turned back to the boarding and stowing of seals.

By 10 A.M. the sealers were well strung out, with Tuff in the lead, and a trail of blackened pinnacles and discarded flagpoles behind them. The going was difficult, the worst ice ever experienced by George Tuff in his eighteen years on the floes. Now, after three hours, a small family of seals was spotted, and the line of men slowed to a crawl.

"A couple men go after them," Tuff ordered, "and haul 'em back to the path. We'll pick up the pelts later."

Four men from Hant's Harbour, Joe Francis, Roland Critch, Ed Short, Charlie Evans, and a Trinity man, Alpheus John Harris, left the line and took off for the seals. They killed and sculpted them while Tuff took another bearing. It was thick to the eastward, and the sky was now obscured by haze. The low pressure depressed them. There was less bantering now, and someone voiced the opinion that bad weather was in the air. Tuff agreed: "There'll be weather ere long. Rain, I 'low."

Joshua Holloway, casting an uneasy eye around, saw with dismay that there was a reddish tinge in the overcast near the sun. Along the line the murmur arose about the sun hounds seen earlier. The uneasiness that had dogged some of them from the beginning was now out in the open. Ice Master Stephen Jordan remarked to his friend Jim Evans that he had seen the sun hounds and a dark cloudbank on the horizon at dawn. "Sun hounds never brought no good, an' the cloudbank says fer an easterly wind," he declared.

Evans agreed. "Let's go back to the ship," he suggested.

"Go back?" Stephen privately thought it a good idea, but he was an ice master, after all, and somewhere ahead in the line he had a young brother, Tom, and two nephews, Henry and Bernard. "I don't know," he said dubiously.

But soon the idea of returning to the ship was tossed around openly. They had walked about four miles over the world's worst ice, and were still miles from the *Stephano*, which was slowly moving off north-westward. Chasing a retreating ship might take all day. Besides, there seemed to be no seals.

"What in hell are we doin' here?" they asked each other.

Up front, Tuff gave the signal to move on, but some of those at the rear of the column did not move. The Hant's Harbour men had got back to the path and stowed their pelts, and were preparing to hurry to catch up when they were met by a column of men returning. A Bonavista Bay fisherman, Tobias Cooper, had been the first actually to turn around and head back for the *Newfoundland*. He was prepared to go alone if necessary. Jim Evans quickly joined him. Then Jordan made his decision. His brother and nephews would have to take their chances. He too turned his face towards their own ship. He noted uneasily that she was enveloped in a dancing haze that played tricks on the eyes.

There were catcalls and shouts of "Cowards," as they began their retreat, but common sense prevailed, and more than twenty men turned back, joining the five men with their small catch of seals.

Alpheus John Harris, at fifty-two the oldest in the group of five, spoke up:

"I'm going back to the *Newfoundland*."

"Shouldn't we ask our master watch?"

"I don't need Tom Dawson to tell me what to do," Harris said. "There's a starm comin' up, an' 'e should be here right now t' lead us back to the ship, but I can get there without 'e's help."

Still towing his seal pelt, he began the return journey to the *Newfoundland*. The other four followed, taking the small catch of pelts with them. In all, thirty-four men turned back.

As the break between the two parties widened, many others in the column wavered. Even the youngest were beginning to lose their nerve, seeing their weather-wise elders so uneasy. But Cecil Mouland was astonished that they should even think of turning back. "A cowardly thing to do!" he declared, and firmly believed that it was.

Still murmuring about the weather, they went on. They were nearer the *Stephano* now than to their own ship, and this kept them going.

Two Bonavista Bay men, fifty-one-year-old Alfred Maidment and his thirty-one-year-old brother, Bob, were predicting dire things.

"Remember the *Greenland*," Alfred sid.

"Them men warn't so far from their ship as we be now," Bob agreed. "'Twill be all right if we can get aboard the *Stephano*."

Joshua Holloway, who had a brother, Philip, in the line a-head, felt they ought to turn back. All the signs spoke of an impending storm.

"We should've gone back with the first crowd," Joshua said to his companion, Jesse Collins.

"We can still go," Jesse said.

But Joshua couldn't bring himself to leave without his brother, and of course there was no way to pass word ahead to him. Just the same, he stopped: "We should go back. I know it."

A group, including the two Maidments, collected around Holloway and Collins. They were all experienced sealers, aware of the danger they were in.

Jesse Collins said, "If ye go back, I'll go with you. If ye go on, I'll follow."

The final decision lay with Joshua Holloway. He turned to Alfred Maidment. "What do you think?"

He considered. "The *Stephano* is handier," he pointed out. "It'll take us longer to get to the *Newfoundland*." This was undeniable, so he made the decision for them all: "If the rest of the fellers can do it, we can." They went forward under the gathering storm.

Nearer the front of the column John Howlett was walking with Master Watch Dawson and Lemuel Squires. Though Howlett was in Sidney Jones's watch, he had formed a close friendship with Dawson. Now Howlett, regretting his decision to go out on the ice instead of crawling into his bunk early that morning, suggested to Dawson that they ought to go back to the ship. Dawson wouldn't even consider it, and Howlett wouldn't go back without him.

Some miles to the north-north-west, the *Stephano*'s crew had done a hard morning's work killing and panning seals, keeping an eye, now and then, on the threatening signs in the sky. There was not a live seal left in their vicinity, which was a relief to Sam Horwood, an experienced fishing skipper from Carbonear, who knew a gathering storm when he saw it. He wasted no time in going to the ice master, David Dove. "We got all the swiles scraped together; we can do no more around here; let's get back to the ship," he urged.

But David Dove did not have the authority to return to the ship unless their master watch, John Kelloway, gave the order. Kelloway was with another party, farther north.

"That's where we've got to head for," Dove argued. "North to Skipper John."

"If that gale ye can see brewin' to the south-east comes on as quick as I expect it will, and the ice stretches abroad, as it most likely will, we're liable to be out here for the night," Horwood warned.

"If we was to go back and Kelloway was to find more seals, an' us not there to lend a hand, ye know we'd catch hell from the Old Man," Dove argued.

The thought of catching hell from the Old Man made even such a tough nut as Skipper Sam Horwood pause.

"There's no denyin' that," he agreed. "All right, b'y, let's go find Kelloway."

"If it comes too bad to get to the *Stephano*, we're not so far from the *Florizel*," Dove pointed out.

The thought was not much comfort to Sam Horwood. The *Florizel* and the *Bonaventure* were closer, true, but the ice between the men and the ships was rough.

Farther north-west another small group of sealers brought their last tow of pelts to a pan and stopped for a blow, wiping their bloodied, greasy faces with bloodied, greasy hands.

"That's the lot, Skipper," Mark Sheppard said.

Mark was a St. John's man, in his fourth year at the hunt, but serving for the first time with Abram Kean. They had been on the ice since dawn, had cleaned up their patch, and now were ready for more.

"Lots of 'em up-along, boys." James Morgan, the ice master waved north-west, where whitecoats still lay in profusion. Mark, Dan Foley, Ambrose Conway, and Stan Samson needed no further encouragement. They were exhausted, but this was what they had come to the ice for. Coiling their greasy tow ropes they headed north-north-west.

The storm was now tearing across the centre of the Grand Banks, sucking in furious winds as it came. Near the eye of the storm a deluge of rain was falling, but all around its edges, where the air mass had lost some of its heat by sucking in cold winds from the flanking high pressure regions, the moisture was drifting down in blinding curtains of snow. The snow was caught by the cool winds being sucked into the coil, and driven in blinding gusts. Cape Breton and the entire south coast of Newfoundland were numbed by the blizzard. The first flakes of snow were falling over St. John's.

Down around the south-east corner of Newfoundland, well to the west of Cape Race, a heavy sea was running, and the air was thick with snow.

The S.S. *Portia* was about five miles west-south-west of Cape Pine, carrying mail and passengers, bound eastward for Trepassey. But since a blizzard was coming on, and it was not safe to round Cape Pine without plenty of sea room in such conditions, Captain Thomas Conners had decided to run up St. Mary's Bay for shelter. There was shoal ground seaward from the cape, and treacherous Freels Rock lay two miles off shore. With a swell heaving in like this the seas would be dangerous a long way from shore, building up over the shallow ocean bed to short, steep waves that might cause a ship to founder.

As he and his chief officer stood on the bridge discussing the probable course of the wind (it was "backing" from south to east, and would be northerly later, before coming east again), they were startled by an apparition that came looming out of the snow. It was a big ship, making "heavy weather" with her scuppers rolling into the swells, and she barely missed cutting the *Portia* in two, passing within a cable-length of her stern.

"It's the *Southern Cross*!" Captain Conners exclaimed. He saluted with a blast of his whistle. The sealing ship sounded her siren in reply. She was racing east-north-east towards Cape Race.

At 10:30 A.M. Navigator Charles Green on the *Newfoundland* noted that the barometer was still falling.

At 10:40 Captian Abram Kean on the *Stephano* saw that the *Newfoundland*'s crew was trying to reach him, so he ordered his ship to turn about. Shouting for the chief cook, who appeared promptly, he told him to get on kettles of tea. He had already made the decisions on behalf of the men from the *Newfoundland*:

"We'll pick 'em up, give 'em some grub, an' take 'em back to that patch of swiles we left on our port side," he told Yetman.

Meanwhile the cooks had disappeared below to put out bags of hard tack and boil kettles of tea.

At eleven o'clock the crew of the *Florizel* had just about cleaned up the patch of seals they were working in the heavy ice, when Joe and his brother Nathan noticed that whitecoats lay to the westward of the *Stephano*. They rightly concluded that seals must be even more plentiful to the north-west, where the *Stephano*'s men were working. Joe ordered his crews aboard, but left six men finishing up a patch of seals eastward from his ship.

"They'll be safe. Father'll be around for some considerable time," he told his brother.

Both had noticed that the *Newfoundland*'s men were now about a mile from the *Stephano*, and that she was slowly working towards them. They went off north-west, finally passing the last of the *Stephano*'s men, and putting their own men on the ice beyond them. There were plenty of seals in that direction, and it was still perfectly safe for men to work on the ice so long as there was a ship near by.

The *Bonaventure*, having made a good kill by following the *Florizel* the day before, got up steam and headed off in her wake.

At this time, too, some of the *Stephano*'s men, taking warning from the lowering sky, shifting wind and loosening ice, began to head south-east in her direction. It was obvious, now, that weather was coming on fast.

The storm, drawing tremendous energy from its own condensing moisture, had raced with terrific speed across the Avalon Peninsula of Newfoundland. A few short flurries had fallen over St. John's, and then, with amazing suddenness, the city was wrapped in a raging blizzard. Within half an hour everything had come to a stop, and the city was "snowed in" while the drifts began to pile up to the eaves of the houses.

Over the ice-field, a hundred miles north of St. John's, the first flakes began to fall.

# CHAPTER EIGHT

The *Newfoundland*'s men were still in the heavy ice at eleven o'clock and Dawson stopped for a short breather closer by one of the *Stephano*'s flags. It was the one that had been left there the day before when the Old Man had abandoned the handful of seals in that vicinity for the large herd on the sheet ice to the west. The flag was identified as the *Stephano*'s by its crimson colour. (There was a number on it, but whether it was 198 or 189 was later a matter of dispute.)

Dawson and several of his buddies, taking time out for a snack of hard tack, had more interest in the weather. That snow or rain was about to fall was obvious from the veiled sky and the rawness of the wind. "What kind o' board d'ye get on the *Stephano*, I wonder?" he mused aloud, adding, "If she's not our boarding house tonight, b'ys, I'm a good piece out."

The crimson flag fluttered over the handful of pelts and only two men observed another flag about half a mile farther west. Only Joshua Holloway distinguished its crimson colour and concluded that it was another *Stephano* flag. Cecil Tiller saw the flag, but to him it was just another flag, ownership unknown. This was to be an important issue, later.

As they continued towards the *Stephano* the ice smoothed a little, making the walk easier. But it was too good to last. Now, after a morning scrambling over solid rafted ice they were in ice that floated free, forcing them to jump from pan to pan. Several suffered wet feet and legs when a pan crumbled beneath the onslaught of so many boots. But this happened all the time among sealers and little was thought about it. On board ship their wet feet would soon dry out. And the *Stephano*, they saw, was steaming towards them.

The haze thickened and Thomas Dawson again spoke of the *Stephano* as their boarding house for the night. Many others were of the same mind. They had travelled not four or five miles, as estimated by Tuff and Wes Kean, but closer to six or seven. The warmth of the day plus the long, difficult scramble over and around rough ice-floes had wearied them.

They were quite sure their billet for the night would indeed be the *Stephano*. Only Benjamin Piercey disagreed. "Look, b'ys, we bin walkin' all day and seen only four, five swiles, so why should Cap'n Kean keep us aboard the *Stephano* for the night? It'd be more to the point if he took us back to the *Newfoundland*."

Most of them agreed with Ben, and most would have been gratified to get a run back to their ship after that tortuous walk. They were used to walking, sure, but ice travel was a horse of a different colour, and they were bloody tired. So they went on, quite satisfied that if *Stephano* didn't keep them aboard, she would surely take them back to their own ship.

Although the sky was veiled, it was still a soft, gentle day. At approximately 11:20 A.M. the first pecks of snow began to fall; at that same time the *Stephano* and the *Newfoundland*'s crew met on the edge of the heavy ice near where the *Florizel* had been working earlier.

On the *Stephano*'s bridge, Captain Kean was joined by Second Hand Yetman. "Didn't take 'em long to get to us, Cap'n," he remarked.

The Old Man grunted. "When they're all aboard, steam in around the p'int of big ice to where we left the flag last evenin', Fred," he said to Yetman. Then he leaned over the bridge and bellowed, "Come aboard, me sons, I'll give ye yer dinner and put ye on to a spot of swiles."

The *Stephano* didn't stop. Ken merely slowed her to a crawl to let the men grab the crude side sticks that served as ladders. Agile as monkeys, the sealers swarmed up the side sticks and over the railing. The last men on the ice had to run to keep up with her before they had the chance to grab a stick. John Hiscock was one of these men, and he was angry when he finally landed on her deck, amid all the other sealers milling about looking for a place to ease their tired bodies. But the Old Man greeted Hiscock and the others with a roar, "Hurry up, me sons, get below and get your mug-up. Be as quick as ye can."

Captain Kean was in a hurry. Within minutes, the *Stephano* had turned and was steaming westward to get around the bulge of heavy ice. Deck hands were already directing the *Newfoundland*'s crew below to the holds.

Northward, the group from the *Stephano*, consisting of Mark Sheppard, Stanley Samson, James Morgan, Daniel Foley, and Ambrose Conway, took their bearing as the snow began to fly. They set their course with a compass, by the line of flags that extended almost in a straight line to the south-south-east. The *Stephano* had gone away to the east when they started back, but presently she was steaming away westerly, crossing their line of flags and gradually disappearing from view in the thickening weather.

They halted, "*Now*, where's she goin'?"

"Maybe she's putting out more men," one suggested.

"With weather comin' on? Nah!"

"Then where's she goin'?"

None of them could hazard a guess. Everyone on board except the deck hands needed to sail her had been dropped on the ice; had the Old Man picked up the first watch to drop them farther south? It didn't seem logical. "Wherever she's gone," Mark summed up, "she's gone fer some purpose."

There was no arguing with that.

They kept walking south-east.

In the barrel of the *Newfoundland*, Captain Wes Kean had watched his men through the spy-glass. He had climbed the mast to the barrel at 7 A.M. as his men left the ship and had stayed there to watch and worry. He had watched the long, thin line of men snaking around the rugged ice-floes; he had waited patiently as the men halted periodically to take their bearings, and he was still there at ten o'clock when the group on the tail end of the column broke away and did not continue with the others.

From the bridge, Charles Green had called, "Looks like a watch crew is stayin' behind to pan seals, Cap'n."

Had they come upon a patch of seals?

He could see no evidence of seals. In fact, the men appeared to be doing nothing at all, and only after what seemed a great length of time did they begin to return along the trail they had made going over the ice. Obviously they were coming back to the *Newfoundland*.

Practically one full watch returning. Wes was furious; what the devil did they think they were doing?

The light south-east wind baffled occasionally to the west and back again; to the south and east the sky was thickening gradually and Wes, still angry at the group headed towards him, felt a growing anxiety for the main group moving so slowly northward. It was pecking snow when he saw them finally reach the *Stephano* and begin to board her. He breathed a heartfelt prayer of relief.

He stayed there, the spy-glass glued to his eye, watching his men board the *Stephano*. But presently the snow thickened and the *Stephano* was not so easily seen.

At that point, the steward poked his head out on the bridge and called, "Dinner, Cap'n!"

Wes, with one last look in the direction of the *Stephano*, came down from the barrel and entered the dining room. Green was already seated. "Our men are aboard of the *Stephano*," Wes told him shortly. Then he turned to the steward, "Tell the bo'sun to take the bearin's of the *Stephano* fer me."

Seating himself at the table, Wes told Green, "The weather's gettin' thicker, but our b'ys will be all right aboard the *Stephano*. Father will look out fer 'em."

With a clear conscience, he tackled his heavy hot dinner.

The steward passed Kean's order to the bo'sun, John Tizzard, who immediately went to the bridge. He could still distinguish the *Stephano* through the falliing snow and took her bearings: north-west by north. He could see no sign of activity; no men on the ice. The *Stephano* did not appear to be moving.

When George Tuff had climbed aboard the *Stephano* with the rest of the *Newfoundland*'s crew, he had been greatly relieved to be aboard ship again. Until someone passed on the information, he had been unaware that part of his crew had turned back, and even then was much too busy to worry about it. Now as Abram Kean bellowed at Tuff's men to hurry, Tuff spoke to Master Watch Dawson, "Better see that your men get somethin' to eat, Tom."

Dawson, in bad humour after the long walk, replied, "I'm damned if I will. I don't have any authority on this ship."

Tuff didn't have time to argue. He moved hurriedly off to join Captain Kean on the bridge. You didn't keep the Old Man waiting.

The crowd of exhausted sealers on the *Stephano*'s deck was thinning as the men were gradually, urgently directed by the deck hands into the holds. But Richard McCarthy, Joseph Hiscock, Benjamin Leary, and Lemuel Squires were still looking around the *Stephano* in awe. The large passenger ship was a beauty and it might well be their one and only time aboard her; that curved stem that let her ride upon the ice could make any man fall in love with her.

But Tuff's voice crackled from the bridge, "Never mind gazin' around, hurry up and get a mug-up or you'll do without it."

They moved towards the hold, muttering and throwing hostile looks towards Tuff. But they were choking for a drink of tea anyway, so they went below to one of the holds where throngs of their mates clumped about hungrily, waiting for dinner. Of course there was no one to wait on them; they had to dig for themselves among the food that had been prepared. Some managed to get hot tea with their hard tack, others had to be content with cold tea with it; and some did without tea because there wasn't enough tea or mugs to go around. A few, more adventurous (and less honest) than the others, poked around and actually found someone's private cache of boiled beans.

Meanwhile, Dawson went below, not to the officers' mess with the rest of the master watches, because no one directed him there, but to the hold where most of his watch had been directed. He and a handful of men didn't need to fill themselves with hard tack, since they had eaten some half an hour earlier on the ice.

But despite the shortage of tea, Dawson managed to get a mug. Before he could drink, complaints were voiced by the remainder of his men; beside him a young fellow complained that he was "chokin'" for a drink, and Dawson handed him his tea. "Here, b'y." Then he left the milling, complaining men and went topside.

Master Watches Mouland, Bungay, and Jones were invited to the officers' dining room for meat, potatoes, and turnip hash. Bungay and Jones took a leisurely break, asking George Yetman, the Old Man's private cook, to keep an eye out and let them know when their men were leaving ship. Mouland ate hurriedly and returned topside to prowl the deck of the *Stephano* and keep an eye out for Tuff. Efficient and sure of himself, Mouland was eager to get on with the sealing.

The *Stephano*, he noticed, was steaming south-west.

In the holds, the sealers learned through the grapevine that they were heading for a patch of seals "to the south-west." The exact position was not given to them, but the general impression was "south-west," particularly since it was reported to them that the *Stephano* was at present steaming in that direction.

But it came as an unpleasant surprise to some of them to learn that they had to go right back on the ice. A man here and there decided not to, and slipped quietly away to seek a hiding place. John Howlett was one of them.

Dawson, meantime, sat on the forehatch and began to fill his pipe. There he was joined by John Hiscock, second master watch. "Did ye get a mug-up, Skipper?" he asked Dawson.

Dawson grunted, "No!"

"Never mind, the tea's cold anyway. 'Tis not much of a dinner they're givin' us."

Dawson agreed. "I don't need a cup of tea *that* bad."

Hiscock hunched his shoulders against the wind and snow. "'Tis a pretty dirty day, now."

Dawson growled, "Yah! and it's gettin' worse."

They sat on the hatch as Dawson tried to light his pipe, but the wind was striking the ship on the port quarter and they found it too windy and snowy for comfort. They got up and sought shelter on the starboard side of the ship, waiting for orders. While Dawson lit his pipe, Hiscock took out his own pocket compass and noted the ship's direction, which was approximately west-south-west. It did not occur to him that his cheap little compass might be affected by the magnetic influence of the steel ship—not that it would have mattered a great deal, for even without checking with his compass he was pretty sure they were heading generally south-west.

Tuff had been met by Captain Kean. Navigator William Martin saw him take the second hand towards the dining room and heard him remark about the nice patch of seals they had passed that morning, before the captain and Tuff moved out of his bearing.

In the captain's dining room Tuff removed his snow goggles for the first time since leaving the *Newfoundland*. The two men spoke briefly of the weather, agreeing that while it was "dirty" weather, it was soft and mild and the glass was still fair—still above 29, and that was "a fine weather glass" as far as Abram Kean was concerned—typical spring weather. They got down to business while Tuff ate the dinner put before him. He told the Old Man about the *Newfoundland*'s difficulties since leaving

Wesleyville; and about the lamentable lack of seals. "Well," said the Old Man, "after y'e ve had yer dinner I'll put ye on to a spot of seals where ye can pan a thousand or more and go on board o' yer own ship, George."

This was totally unexpected and threw Tuff into a quandary. Go on board their own ship? He had fully expected that he and his crew would remain on the *Stephano* for the night. But the Old Man apparently had other ideas and Tuff knew well that subordinates did not readily oppose the Old Man's ideas. He said, "Well, sir, Cap'n Wes told me that 'e wouldn't give me any instructions, but I should come t'you and you'd tell me all about the swiles an' where to go."

"An' I will, George."

The Old Man told him that the seals lay in a string that ran from the north-north-west to the south-south-east and was probably not more than half a mile wide. "The main body lies to the north-north-west in a narrow string and already the *Florizel*'s crew have gone to the westward o' my crew, and the *Bonaventure* is goin' in now with all her men to the westward o' the *Florizel*'s men, and I don't think ye can reach any swiles in that direction without goin' ten or twelve miles from yer ship, *which is too far*, George."

George nodded. There was no disputing that.

The Old Man continued. "I left a little spot o' fourteen or fifteen hundred swiles which you can pan, and I've instructed my second hand to steam out there while yer men are eating. We'll steam to where we struck a flag for a mark last evening. It'll be a fine guide for you. Ye'll then be two miles nearer yer own ship than when I picked ye up, me son, and ye can get aboard yer own ship afore night."

George kept his thoughts to himself. Earlier, looking at the *Stephano* from the barrel of the *Newfoundland*, he had thought that the *Stephano*'s men were killing in the vicinity of the ship and that the *Newfoundland*'s men would be able to do the same; he had assumed that when the *Stephano*'s men boarded their ship at the end of the day, so would the *Newfoundland*'s men. Now it was all changed. The *Stephano*'s men were miles away to the north-west; there were no seals left to be killed in the immediate vicinity, only the seals the Old Man had left untouched, southward, two miles nearer their own ship. It put a different light on the situation. Tuff said nothing, but frowningly concentrated on finishing his meal quickly.

Abram Kean was not a man to waste time. "If ye're finished, George, I want ye to get yer crew underway. We have to get back to our work as quickly as possible, because some o' my men must be five or six miles from us now."

Tuff rose hastily. "I don't want to delay you, sir," he said, and followed Captain Kean to the bridge. The Old Man roared, "All hands out!" He dispensed orders to his deck hands to get below and get the *Newfoundland*'s men topside.

As the men assembled hastily on deck, he said to Tuff, "The swiles lay two miles to the south-west." Then he signalled to the ship's compass, "Take her bearings, George."

The ship had steamed around the bulge of heavy ice, dodging east and west to avoid heavy pans. It was still mild, though getting rawer, and the snow had thickened, limiting visibility. Tuff, no longer wearing snow goggles, looked vainly for the *Newfoundland*. "Where's our ship, sir?" he asked.

The Old Man pointed south-east, "There she is, George, bearing due south-east."

Tuff still couldn't see her. Maybe it was because he'd been wearing goggles all morning, he thought. The ship's compass, he noted, showed that the *Stephano* was heading south-west; the wind was breezing from the south-east.

The Old Man called to Fred Yetman in the barrel, "Fred, can ye see the flag we left here yesterday?"

Yetman called back, "There 'tis, Cap'n, jest a little on our port bow."

About half a mile off the port bow, in the south-east quarter, the flag of the *Stephano* fluttered in the breeze, still visible through the snow.

Since no other ship had been in this vicinity, Captain Kean and his second hand were both convinced that this was the flag they had planted the day before in the big ice. They were unaware of a second flag that they had overlooked earlier that morning, the one noticed by Joshua Holloway and Cecil Tiller as they passed by the flag in the big ice. Abram Kean was taking the men half a mile farther westward than he thought.

Tuff, glancing over the ship's side, saw that the ice was slack to windward, and that there wasn't a large enough pan near by for his men to jump to in safety. But the Old Man was two steps ahead of him. He roared, "Hard-a-starboard!" Since she was heading south-west in a south-east wind, the starboard was in the lee. The bow swung into the ice, forced it tightly together, and gave the men solid footing in the lee of the ship.

"All hands out," George shouted, and went to the deck, hurrying his men over the side. He was one of the first on the ice.

Watching from the bridge, Captain Kean roared, "All hands out on the starboard side, and hurry it up . . . cross 'er head, b'ys."

Flagpoles and gaffs were thrown hastily to the ice, and then the men jumped. They went willingly, confident that their leader, George Tuff, had made arrangements for their welfare. All were looking forward to returning to spend a night on the big, beautiful *Stephano*.

There was one disaster. Thirty-three-year-old Benjamin Piercey, still tired after the walk over the ice, stated flatly, "If anyone'll stay with me, I won't leave."

His friends rallied around, urging him to stay with his own, and with great reluctance he went over the side with them. The men who had tried to stow away had been routed by the *Stephano*'s crew, and hustled over the side. They went sullenly.

Since the ship was headed south-west, the men were on the wrong side for seals, and as ordered by Captain Kean, they hurried forward to cross her bow. Tuff, on the ice below the *Stephano*'s bridge, looked with growing apprehension at the thickening snow. He called up to the Old Man, "It looks fer weather, sir."

The Old Man shouted back, "My glass don't show fer weather, George. Now you go south-west a couple of miles, track my carcasses and ye'll find about fourteen hundred swiles. Kill 'em and go on board your own ship." To the last handful of sealers lingering on the deck, he shouted, impatiently, "Hurry up, b'ys, I want to get to my own men."

Those sealers on the ice still within hearing distance of the captain's words heard these orders with great uneasiness. They murmured amongst themselves, "We'll never see the *Newfoundland* this night." But no one raised his voice against the all-powerful Captain Kean. He could never be wrong.

Anyway, there was no point in arguing. Kean was so anxious to get back to his own men. As the last sealer was crossing the bow of the *Stephano*, he had to step lively to avoid being run down. The ship slewed to the starboard, leaving the *Newfoundland* men on her port side, and soon disappeared from view, heading northward.

The crew of the *Newfoundland* felt they had been abandoned, like the stark carcasses of the whitecoats strewing the ice.

Keeping a faithful record of proceedings, William J. Martin noted in the log of the *Stephano*:

*11:30 a.m.* Newfoundland *crew walked on board, had mug-up and went on ice again about 11:50 a.m. Noon: wind infreasing from south-east with light snow, barometer 29.50 and falling.*

With the wind still from the south-east, he estimated that the wind would chop off to the north and quickly moderate.

Aboard the *Newfoundland*, Charles Green wrote in his log:
*Noon: Wind freshening and drifting snow.*
In St. John's, Roper's barograph recorded:
*Noon: 29.10, a drop of 40 tenths in four hours.*

By noon, aboard the *Newfoundland* it was impossible to see any other ship. Knowing that one watch was returning to them, Wes ordered the whistle blown so that his men would not go astray, but he was still nursing his anger against them.

More than a mile away, the men heard the whistle thankfully. They had not relied on the path to bring them back, but had used their compasses. John Harris, Roland Critch, Joseph Francis, Edmund Short, and Charles Evans were still well to the rear, with Charles suffering severe cramps. Their arms ached with the tow of seals, but they did not relinquish them.

To the north-north-west, the *Stephano*'s own men had prudently decided that the time had come to return to their ship. The master watches and ice masters had called their men together and begun to walk in the direction their ship should be. It was beginning to snow in earnest and the icefield was no place for a man to linger.

Mark Sheppard and his fellow sealers were travelling steadily in a south-westerly direction, anxiously alert for any sign of the *Stephano*. They had to concentrate now on the ice beneath their feet, for it was "stretching abroad" too quickly for their liking. If the *Stephano* didn't appear soon, they could be in a lot of trouble.

One hundred and thirty-two sealers of the *Newfoundland* watched the stern of the *Stephano* disappear in the swirling snow, many of them suspecting, for the first time, that she was not coming back for them. Joshua Holloway spoke with finality, "Well, I 'low we're gonna spend a night on the ice."

Bewildered, the men turned to their leader, crowding around him, their fears and anxieties engulfing him completely.

"There's a starm on, George."

"What we doin' here?"

Then an accusation, "George, ye're our leader, ye brought us here."

"What's goin' to happen to we, George?"

The situation, the magnitude of the responsibility, hit George Tuff perhaps for the first time. He was in charge now. He was no longer taking orders from Captain Kean, or from anyone else. There was nobody to take orders from. Slowly he was coming to realize the peril in which they had been placed. The anxious faces, the questioning eyes of the men clustering around him were too much. He was a man of limited capabilities, and to be responsible for them—many of them personal friends—was overwhelming. Tears rolled down his cheeks. "Cap'n Kean give me orders to kill seals an' go back to our own ship," he pleaded.

A murmur went through the crowd and reached Cecil Mouland and his buddies on the outskirts. "Tuff is cryin'," they said in wonderment.

"Yah! Cap'n Kean told 'im we was to kill swiles and go to our own ship."

Cecil was as astounded as the next man. "How we gonna do that in a starm?"

"Sounds like a row goin' on," another broke in.

There *was* a row. A belligerent Dawson was confronting Tuff, "Is the *Stephano* comin' back to pick us up?" Dawson demanded.

Tuff replied simply, "No!"

Everyone was thunderstruck at the bald statement. The general impression that had taken root among them in the course of that long weary morning, with the weather slowly worsening, was that their home for the night would be the *Stephano*. Now here they were, on the ice, miles from nowhere with a storm coming on.

Dawson asked angrily, "Then where are we goin'?"

Tuff was swiftly recovering from the moment of weakness. "Cap'n Kean give me orders to go and pan swiles a couple miles to the sou'west," he explained calmly.

Dawson was blunt. "It's too dirty to go pannin' swiles. Where are we goin' fer the night if the *Stephano*'s not comin' back fer us?"

Tuff replied shortly, "We have to board our own ship."

"But our ship is sou'-*east*," Dawson pointed out, "how are goin' to find her if we have to go a couple miles to the sou'*west*?"

"We'll allow a p'int or two."

Dawson was argumentative. "I've been twenty or more springs to the ice and ye'll want to run it pretty neat to strike a ship on a day like this. She's a mighty small mark to make."

Reuben Crewe, doubly anxious because of Albert John, voiced an objection, "If we got to walk aboard, George, there's no time to kill swiles."

Tuff was angry now. "I got *orders* to pan swiles and return to our own ship."

John Howlett now added his voice to the dissension. "If we lose time huntin' swiles, we'll never see our vessel this night."

"Yah!"

"He's right."

"I'm in command," Tuff roared angrily, "an' no one goes fer the *Newfoundland* till I say so."

"It's too bad to go huntin' fer swiles," Howlett retorted angrily, "we should go fer our ship *now*."

This was mutiny. Tuff turned on Howlett, his face set with anger. Howlett, ever ready for a fight, put up his fists. The stage was set for a vicious knock-down fight there on the ice, with hobnailed boots no doubt soon coming into play. But Dawson and Squires jumped on Howlett. "Don't be a bloody fool," Squires panted, "ye can't go against the second hand."

"Yes, I can." Howlett, crimson with rage, struggled to free himself and get at Tuff. "I'm as good a man as he is."

They held him until he subsided; then he growled, "Lemme alone."

Tuff had no time to waste on quarrelling. His orders from his own captain had been clear: get orders from Abram Kean and follow them, and this was what he intended doing. Now he ordered the men to fall in behind him, and head south-west. There were five hours of daylight left; they had been brought two miles closer to their ship, or so they believed; they should have time to kill seals and return to the *Newfoundland* before nightfall.

The sealers reluctantly fell in line with much muttering and discontent. Tuff was their commanding officer and there was nothing to do but go for the seals. Howlett, glowering and angry, muttered that Tuff was damned wrong; they should be going for the *Newfoundland*, goddammit!

Only a small segment had been within earshot of the disagreement between Tuff, Dawson, and Howlett; but it swept through the crowd, and the youngsters marvelled that someone had dared to question their leader. But, even so, they realized that there was some cause for alarm. Their leader, who had the authority to do with them as he thought fit, had brought them to the middle of nowhere at the beginning of a storm. They had accepted Tuff's authority because he was the second hand—and he had gained that rank by proving that he was a good, capable man; stubborn at times, perhaps, but a man who knew what he was about. Yet here they were, standing on the grinding, treacherous ice-floes on the North Atlantic, feeling the ominious heave of the ocean beneath their boots and the sting of snow on their cheeks. They were at the mercy of the elements, and miles from any ship.

Jesse Collins remarked, significantly, "Well, b'ys, the *Greenland* disaster will be nothing to *this* one."

Off and on, all day, this unpleasant thought had occurred to most of them and they didn't particularly care to be reminded of it. Besides, few of them thought it could ever be that serious. "It's mild, Jesse, it won't come as bad as the *Greenland*, ol' man."

"Naw!" They comforted each other as the soft, thick snow fell upon them.

"You wait an' see," Jesse prophesied.

With Tuff in the lead, they went south-west, following the trail of frozen seal carcasses that had been left by the *Stephano*'s men the evening before. Dawson, Howlett, and the older sealers followed sullenly. To them, each step to the south-west was pure folly—utter disaster. They felt strongly that their only chance of survival was to start for their ship immediately. It was plain common sense.

They had walked less than a mile when, much to Tuff's surprise, they came upon the whitecoats. He had expected to walk another mile at least—the Old Man had definitely stated the seals were two miles to the south-west. The Old Man was bound to know where the seals were—yet it had only been a mile. Surely that didn't mean they had mistakenly been dropped off a mile too far west—a mile farther from the *Newfoundland*. Surely not. He dismissed the idea. "We're on to the swiles, b'ys, kill 'em and stick some flags," he shouted.

Right beside him, Dawson refused outright. "I'm not sticking any goddamn flags and I'm not ordering any of the men in my watch to, either. It's too dirty to be on the ice killing swiles."

Tuff roared, "Bungay!"

The youthful Bungay unquestionably obeyed his leader, ordering his men to kill, and they went after the whitecoats with zeal. To them, so far, it wasn't exactly a lark, but they had youth, energy, and great confidence. Besides, it *was* mild.

As Bungay's men began to spread out he turned to Joshua Holloway and ordered: "Take ten men and go a little farther south-west and begin panning."

But Joshua, bitterly regretting that he hadn't turned back to the *Newfoundland* hours earlier, flatly refused. "No, b'y, the weather's too bad fer pannin'." He had no intention of doing work that would prolong their stay on the ice.

Bungay didn't press him.

There was certainly no great number of seals, not enough to keep his crew busy for any length of time, so Tuff continued south-west for a hundred yards or so and came upon another small patch of seals. But it was only a very small patch, and Tuff halted indecisively. The wind was beginning to gust and the snow was thickening; it was obvious that this was no little flurry that might blow itself out in five or ten minutes. It had all the earmarks of a full-blown blizzard.

The men closed around Tuff, and John Hiscock asked him, "What are we goin' to do?"

Tuff avoided the question. "There's not too many swiles, is there?"

But Hiscock persisted, "Is Cap'n Kean comin' back fer us?"

"No! We go aboard our own ship."

"Hadn't we better get at it, then?" Hiscock prodded.

Tuff was coming around. "The weather is gettin' worse all right," he concluded. "I think we'll have to forget the swiles and make fer our own ship."

Hiscock growled, "Do you know how long it took us to come out from the *Newfoundland*?" He answered his own question grimly, "Five hours! And it'll take us six hours to get back."

Tuff replied doggedly, "Yah, I s'pose it will, but that's all we can do, go fer the *Newfoundland*."

Standing there on the heaving ice, with the world blotted out by driving snow, Lemuel Squires asked, "How're we goin' to find the *Newfoundland* now?"

"We'll find 'er, all right."

"How?"

Tuff explained. From where the *Stephano* had dropped them their ship had been south-east, Captain Kean had said, and they had travelled less than a mile south-west; by travelling south-east by east, they should intersect their own path of that morning within a mile or so of the *Newfoundland*. It was as simple as that.

The men close to Tuff passed the information through the crowd. In spite of the earlier arguments and disagreements, there were still some who did not fully understand the situation. A voice, full of consternation, asked, "But what about the *Stephano*?"

Tuff explained once more, "Look, b'ys, the *Stephano* is five or six miles from us now, farther away from us than the *Newfoundland*, an' that's where we're goin'." He turned to Dawson, "You lead the men, Dawson—walk south-east by east until you pick up the path we came out in this marnin'. You'll have to walk in the wind's eye and hurry as quick as you can. I'm goin' to stay with the hinder men in case they drop too far behind."

Privately, the sealers thought that Tuff should take the lead back to the *Newfoundland*. One of the master watches should have been delegated to the rear, they thought, and Tuff as their leader should be out front; but they kept their own counsel and called to one another, "Come on, fellers, we're goin' aboard."

Others cupped their mittened hands around their mouths and shouted to Bungay and his men a couple of gunshots away, "Come on, b'ys, we're goin' aboard."

Dawson and John Hiscock checked their compasses and laid their course. In spite of the storm, the men were cheerful and happy; it was still mild, and perhaps the snow would soon turn to rain. Bungay and his men were grinning with relief as they came out of the storm. "What steamer are we goin' on?" asked a youngster.

His face was a study when he was told it was the *Newfoundland*. Now everyone was bluntly told to forget the *Stephano*; they had a good walk ahead of them and should get on with it. The march over the ice began with Dawson leading off. As they left, Tuff called, "Put down yer compasses an odd time and see where ye're goin'."

It was getting rougher, and the snow was beginning to drift as the last of the great column of 132 men moved ahead. Sidney Jones, sticking close to the second hand, heard Tuff remark, "I never saw a better chance to be out all night."

It was now approximately 12:45 P.M.

Wes Kean had taken only twenty minutes for dinner before he was back in the *Newfoundland*'s barrel again. The snow was thicker, the *Stephano* was hidden, and the group of men returning to his ship were also lost to view. He was even more annoyed with those men now that he knew that the rest had safely boarded the *Stephano*. With them back aboard there would be fewer of his men out among the seals and therefore fewer seals for his ship. As he waited for them, he could think only in terms of the loss of time and pelts: His annoyance increased.

But the whistle of the *Newfoundland* continued to blast shrilly. Its sound was a welcome one to Stephen Jordan and his companions as they straggled along the path towards their ship. The rough, Arctic ice had afforded them a little protection from the drifting snow, and the blackened ice pinnacles were as good as any beacon; but the last half mile or so to the ship could have been difficult since it was open to the wind and drifting snow, and visibility was limited. That whistle helped.

It was about 1:30 P.M. when they reached the *Newfoundland*, to find their young captain glaring down over the side at them, angry and vocal. "Who gave you authority to come back?" he demanded.

They halted, gazed at one another uncomfortably. None of them attempted to board ship.

"Well?" He was like a sentry challenging them as they shuffled about on the ice.

Stephen Jordan cleared his throat. "No one give us authority, sir, it looked too bad fer a man to be caught out overnight."

There was a rush of explanations. "We didn't see no swiles, sir."

"The first crowd got a good distance ahead, Cap'n, we saw weather comin' on an' . . . well, sir, we didn't see anythin' to go on fer."

Wes Kean was coldly angry. "The weather glass is steady, there's no sign of a storm; why didn't you follow yer master watch? The crowd that went on ahead got on board the *Stephano* an hour ago. I saw 'em go aboard." He continued as they shifted uncomfortably, "If the seals are there, the men on the *Stephano* are workin' 'em now and *you're here doin' nothin'*! Dammit! What are you, a crowd of grandmothers?"

Jordan spoke defensively, "The *Stephano* was steaming away from us, Cap'n, that was one of the reasons we come back."

Wes snapped, "The master watch had the orders, it was your duty to follow. 'Twasn't a hard walk, and you should all have gone on as long as your master went. In future, b'ys, you go where your master watch goes, and you come back when he comes back, and he alone will be responsible."

Like self-conscious schoolboys, the men stared up at him, as Wes continued, heatedly, "I have no objection to a man returnin,' if he's fallen in or hurt himself, or if he feels he's not equal to a walk in the morning 'fore he leaves, he has only to tell me, *but on the ice he must follow his master watch.*" He glowered at them, "Now, tomorrow you'll have to lose another half day in walkin' to the *Stephano* to jine the others, and let me tell you, b'ys, you'll get no money fer the swiles the others are killin'.""

Having delivered this dressing-down, Wes retired to his cabin, and the men climbed aboard and retired quietly to the holds. They liked their young captian, he treated them fair and square and they liked working for him. So it didn't sit well with them to be on the receiving end of a tongue-banging. Other stragglers, following the sound of the whistle, received the sting of his tongue as they boarded later. The last five to climb wearily aboard were the five men with the seal pelts. Luckily for them they saw no sign of their captain.

Instead, they were met by Bo'sun Tizzard who helped them haul the seals aboard. "Anyone comin' behind you?" he asked.

"No, sir, we'm the last."

The whistle of the *Newfoundland* was discontinued, and silence fell over the blurred, snowy scene.

*Newfoundland* log:

*At 1:30 p.m. thirty-four men returned on board, remainder of crew having boarded S.S. Stephano.*

In St. John's, the storm had been in progress since the early forenoon. Winds were already fierce and snow was beginning to choke the streets. In the harbour a heavy undertow was running and vessels riding in the stream had to put out extra anchors to keep from blowing ashore. As it was, the landing stage at Ayre's Cove was being battered by heavy waves and was being slowly destroyed. In The Narrows the seas were breaking right across the entrance; white water seethed and boiled there, making it impossible for any ship to enter or leave port.

Business came to a halt. Street cars tried to plow through snowdrifts, bogged down, and could not be moved. People deserted the shops and the streets and let winter have full sway. Screaming winds blew snow through streets and alleys, piling it against anything that stood upright; fences and gardens disappeared. Of all the storms that had hit the old town that bad winter, *this* was the worst of all.

The *Southern Cross* should have been safely in St. John's by this time, but with the sea heaving in through The Narrows, it was considered likely that she had by-passed St. John's harbour and made for Harbour Grace, in Conception Bay, three hours' run north and west.

One hundred and seventy-eight miles east of Cape Race, the S.S. *Eagle Point*, on her way to St. John's, was forced to lie-to with her bow into the wind. She had left Liverpool twelve days before and had fought storm after storm across the Atlantic. This was her first trip to the port of St. John's; she was under charter for the conveyance of mails to the Allan Lines, whose agents in St. John's were Furness Withy and Co., Ltd. She would be the largest ship ever to enter The Narrows up to that time, being of 5,222 tons gross, 3,307 tons net. In her holds she carried 2,000 tons of cargo as well as mail. She also carried a powerful Marconi wireless apparatus with an effective radius of 500 miles.

For the *Eagle Point* it was going to be a memorable trip.

# CHAPTER NINE

After dropping the *Newfoundland*'s crew, Captain Abram Kean steamed northward. There were still many pans of pelts to be taken aboard. At each he ordered the ship stopped, and the winches squealed and complained as the heavy loads of pelts came dripping over the sides. On the deck the crew cut out the "flippers," tossed them into barrels, and stowed the pelts, with their attached thick layers of fat, as compactly as possible into the wooden pounds that had been built to hold them.

Farther north the thickening snow and gusting wind was sending Joe Kean in search of his men, the *Florizel*'s whistle sounding at short intervals to summon them on board. It had been reported to him that the whitecoats were taking to the water—a sure sign of stormy weather, and he was anxious about his men. He found them quickly, and with his watches aboard he headed south-east to collect the small group he had left in the heavy ice. Later, when it stopped snowing, he would put his men on the ice again, but not until the bad weather had blown itself out.

Steaming as fast as conditions allowed, Joe found himself at noon among the *Stephano*'s men, marching south-east in search of their ship, some of them now in a state of great anxiety. He slowed to a crawl and shouted for them to come on board. Gratefully, they swarmed up the sides, and were told to go below for dinner. Master Watch Garland Goulton went to the officers' mess, the others to the holds.

The snow was now gusting in blinding drifts, and Joe's thoughts turned not only to the small party he had left behind, but also to his brother's crew, whom he had last seen on the ice about two hours ago. They were a long distance from their ship, but he reckoned that they must be somewhere near the *Stephano*.

He was still some miles from the place he had left his men. It would be safer, he decided, and would save time for everybody, if he continued to pick up his father's crew, and at the same time asked the Old Man to pick up his small party—and the men from the *Newfoundland*.

Going directly to the wireless shack he gave his operator, Patrick Barkley, a verbal message: "Tell the operator of the *Stephano* to ask father to look after my men and the men from the *Newfoundland*. We'll pick up *his* crew. Tell him I left a few men panning seals in the big ice where we were this morning."

"Righto, Captain!" Barkley got to work at once, tapping out the message. Since there was no written copy, this would be one of the numerous "unofficial" messages that captains sent between ships. Joe Kean returned to the bridge with an easy mind.

Somehow, Joe's message was altered a little by the time it reached the Old Man—or at least that is what the Old Man said, later. The message that the *Stephano*'s operator wrote down as it came over the wireless could never be found, but the Old Man remembered it as "You look after my men and I'll look after yours. Small party from *Florizel*, left in big ice this morning." There was no mention of the *Newfoundland*. Of that he was certain.

"Tell 'im ahl rate," the Old Man growled, and the message was flashed back.

Abram Kean now sounded his whistle and kept a sharp lookout for Joe's men. The ice was well "stretched abroad" by now. This made it easy for the ship to manoeuvre but hard for the men on foot to get to her through the loose ice. So wake lines were kept ready to toss to men in loose ice. Soon the *Stephano* was rung down to "stand by" as the Old Man spied a group off the port bow. The lines snaked towards the men, but they made no effort to grab them. He was annoyed.

"What d'ye think ye're doin'?" he roared.

"We're not yer men, sir; we belong to the *Florizel*."

"Come aboard when ye're told!" the Old Man thundered, and the lines were thrown again. With the lines they hauled their pan to the ship's side and climbed the sidesticks.

"The ice-master will come up to the bridge," the captain ordered.

A burly sealer hurried to the bridge.

"What's yer name, me son?"

"Bob Noseworthy, sir, from Pouch Cove."

"Is that all of ye, now? There's none others on the ice?"

"Not in our party, sir. All the rest was aboard with Captain Joe."

"Ah! rate then. Go get some dinner. Ye're to stay aboard till we get alongside the *Florizel*."

Noseworthy and his men disappeared thankfully below, and the *Stephano* steamed slowly north-west, halting occasionally to hoist on board a pan of pelts. Dirty weather it might be, but it wasn't bad enough to stop the Old Man's swilin!

In the vast wilderness of the ice-field, miles from any ship, the crew of the *Newfoundland* snaked slowly over floes that now wheeled and tilted under their feet, as the heavy swell rolled beneath the ice. They could see very little as damp, soft snow swirled around them, blew into their faces, and stuck to eyebrows and beards.

George Tuff, at the rear, ordered those in front not to get too far ahead. It was in his mind to keep a check on the flagpoles the men were so thoughtlessly throwing away. The *Newfoundland*'s stock of flags was small enough, and he might be able to salvage them, but he found the problems of travel now taking his full attention.

There were 132 men trudging along, facing into the wind and snow. The large number slowed the march, and at last Tuff called a halt.

"We're goin' too slow, men. At this rate we'll never get aboard our ship tonight." He turned to Sidney Jones: "Sid, you and your men break off to the nor'ard and travel in line with us. That should speed us up a bit. Keep an eye out for our old path."

There was momentary confusion as the men split into two groups, and annoyance too, when some were undecided whom to follow. There was an altercation, and Lemuel Squires asked Tuff, "Who are we supposed to follow?"

"It don't matter who you follow," Tuff said bluntly, "as long as you keep movin'."

"Do *you* know where we're going'?" Squires asked angrily.

"What odds is it to you?" Tuff demanded.

"Lots of odds, George. My life is as sweet as any man's, and I want to know what course we're going."

Tuff roared in exasperation: "If ye don't like what I'm doin,' Lem, ye can go off an' perish be yerself!"

"That I won't do, George. I just want to know what we're up to."

"Listen, b'y . . ." Tuff pointed ahead. "*I* could travel on board that one in three hours."

"If you can, I can follow you," Squires said. Then he put into words what a lot of them were thinking. "Anyway, that's where ye should be—out front, pickin' the lead fer us."

The accusation was lost on Tuff. He ordered the men on, again warning the leaders not to lose touch with those behind. Fuming, Lemuel Squires stayed with the main group under Dawson.

"Ye should have let me give 'im a poke in the snoot!" Howlett growled. He voiced the feelings of quite a few.

The slow march continued, with much ominous muttering.

"The *Greenland* disaster will be nothing to this one!" Jesse Collins vowed again, repeating a prophecy he had made many times that day.

In actual fact, they did not know exactly where they were going. Dawson, distrustful of Tuff's directions, kept trending a little to the left, more easterly than he had been instructed. This way, he knew, they were certain to come to the edge of the heavy Arctic ice, and to intersect their morning path at some point or other, even if it was farther from their ship than Tuff intended. But Dawson was not going to risk the danger of missing the path altogether.

Suddenly it was not just snowing and blowing. It was a savage blizzard, roaring out of the south-east. The shrill blast of a ship's whistle came to them.

"The *Stephano*!" one man exclaimed. "Whistlin' 'er crew on board because o' the starm."

No one suggested that they make for the *Stephano*. Old Man Kean had ordered them to head for their own ship, and the Old Man's orders were the law of God to the sealers.

If Tuff was right, they should intersect the path about a mile and a half north-west of the *Newfoundland*. So far, they had been walking on fairly flat ice, where their main problem was open water rather than hummocks. In the morning their path out had been through the hummocky Arctic ice. As soon as they reached that ice, all of them were safe, they would find the path and be on board the *Newfoundland* in no time.

Then they came to the edge of the Arctic ice, and the lead men scrambled eagerly over the barrier. Soon, above the noise of the storm, the cry came back from Dawson, "Here's the path!" Their troubles seemed to be over.

It was now approximately 2:30 P.M., and they could see the first of their abandoned flagpoles from the morning.

The *Stephano* had continued north-west, picking up pelts. The dirty weather did not bother the Old Man. It was a flurry that would soon turn to rain, of that he felt sure. He did not change his mind until the blizzard struck them with apocalyptic fury. Then he ordered the bo'sun to sound the ship's whistle on the chance that some of his men might be nearby.

"Get the Marconi operator," he said.

George Shecklin appeared on the bridge.

"Ask the *Florizel* if our men be aboard."

Shecklin hurried to the wireless shack while the Old Man kept his eyes glued to the trail of flayed seal carcasses, marking the route his ship had followed that day. Any men on the ice would be somewhere along this trail. He spotted some men off the port bow just as Shecklin returned to the bridge.

"All but one watch on board, Cap'n Joe says, sir. George March's crew are still on the ice."

"Ahl rate, me son, we've found 'em. Now ye tell Cap'n Joe to head t'wards me. Slow, mind! An' e's to kape 'e's whistle soundin' an' I'll do likewise."

Shecklin again vanished while the Old Man got the watch on board and made sure they were all accounted for. Three others, George March reported, were still on the ice, "about two hundred yards to win'ard." One had fallen all the way into the water and was having a hard time of it, he said. He had left two men to help him when they heard the whistle.

A slight change of course brought the three sealers in sight, and the exhausted man, drenched with ice water, was hoisted up the side. The others climbed thankfully aboard. All the men of the *Stephano* and the *Florizel* were now accounted for.

Mark Sheppard was with George March's watch, the last to be picked up, and when he went below for dinner he heard for the first time from a fellow sealer, Mike Fowlow, about the *Newfoundland*'s men.

"Ye're mistaken, Mike," Mark said, thirstily gulping tea. "'Tis the *Florizel*'s men we got aboard."

Fowlow shook his head. "There's no mistake, Mark. The whole *Newfoundland* crew was on board this one fer a lunch, then they was put out killin' swiles."

Sheppard's eyes widened. "Ye mean they're still on the ice? Where would they be now?"

"That's what we'd like to know."

No one could say where they were, but all were certain of one thing—they weren't anywhere near the *Newfoundland*.

Mark finished his dinner, put on a heavy jacket, and went topside to help load pelts. It did not occur to him or anyone else on the *Stephano* just then to go to Captain Abram Kean and ask about the *Newfoundland*'s men. If they were still on the ice, then of course the Old Man had arranged with some ship to have them picked up.

It was only later that they discovered that he hadn't even mentioned them to anyone.

In the small Salvation Army school at Doting Cove young Jessie Collins was busy teaching her class. The snow had been heavy since noon, and around three o'clock a sudden gust of wind struck the door, driving it open with a crash that startled the whole class. She hurried to close it with a shiver, and just then Cecil Mouland's cheerful face seemed to come before her eyes. She tried to go back to her duties, but the face of her husband-to-be kept haunting her, filling her with alarm. Try as she would, she could not dismiss Cecil from her mind.

Among the *Newfoundland*'s men there was jubilation. They had found the path, the highway to home, and now all they had to do was retrace their steps! Soon they would be on board, gulping kettles of hot tea! The *Newfoundland*, they believed, was only a mile or so away. With three and a half hours of daylight remaining, a well-marked path, their task would be easy, in spite of the blizzard.

But they had walked only a few hundred yards when they received a nasty shock. Beside the path was a crimson flag, with the number 198.

It was the *Stephano*'s flag, the one they had passed that morning, a good four hours out from the *Newfoundland*.

"Lard Jesus! Ye sartin 'tis the same one?"

"Aye! 'Tis the same number. An' there be jest five, six pelts. It gotta be the same flag. There be neither other flag on the path."

"What's all the jawin' about?" the stragglers were asking.

"Somethin' wrong here, b'ys."

"We won't be gettin' aboard accardin' to *that*!"

There was really great alarm now. They were dog-tired, lashed by a blizzard, and had at least four hours to go over some of the worst ice in the world. If the *Stephano had* brought them a couple of miles nearer their ship, she would have brought them to this point, even a mile or so to the south of it. As it was, they had travelled south-east by east from the seals. If Captain Kean *had* dropped them where he said, how could they have possibly walked for nearly two hours and got to this point, especially travelling by compass?

Tuff's suspicions, aroused when first the patch of seals had appeared earlier than the Old Man had predicted, had been fulfilled. "Well, b'ys," he said grimly, "it looks like Cap'n Kean took us further west than 'e thought 'e did. No use frettin' about it now. We're on the path at any rate."

Dawson did not volunteer the information that he had been falling off a point or two towards the left. He had brought them to the path; finding it justified his action, he thought. To him it was a personal triumph to have brought the party to a point on the ice-field where at least they knew where they were.

No one, apparently, thought of staying there for the night, even though they had seal pelts that they could burn, carcasses near by that they could eat, ice cakes and wet snow to build a shelter—and were in a place where the *Stephano* might find them. They started for the *Newfoundland* without a murmur, even though they knew they could not reach her until some time after dark.

"You lead, Dawson," Tuff ordered, "and keep the wind on yer left cheek."

Driving snow almost blinded them, but the path, protected by hummocks and rafters, could still be seen. The blackened ice pinnacles were good markers. If they could just stick to the path, and it did not become buried by the drifts, they were sure to find their ship, no matter how late. . . .

But currents and winds now began to play havoc with the ice. The smaller pans started to wheel and circulate, moving the trail and making it hard to follow. Dawson, the real leader at this stage, directed some of the men to take up a zig-zag course, reporting flagpoles or blackened ice pinnacles whenever they saw them. In this way they managed to keep on a fairly straight path for the *Newfoundland*.

The heavy snow was not drifting much. It was too wet for that, but in places it lay knee-deep and was very exhausting to Dawson and those near him who were also breaking trail. He was now ready to drop from weariness, but having been ordered to take the lead could not delegate it to anyone else.

Howlett, sticking close to Dawson, spoke out angrily, "Dammit! What's wrong with Tuff? Why don't he tell someone else to take the lead? He's goin' t'have us out all night."

The long black column crept south-east. Then, at the rear, William Pear began to fall behind. An inexperienced sealer, Pear was so nearsighted that he had to wear heavy glasses. In the blizzard they were constantly coated with snow. He could not see with them or without them. And he was feeling sick, besides. He sank to the snow. Tuff ordered a halt until he could catch up.

"Thank God!" Dawson muttered, getting out cakes of hard tack for a much-needed snack. All along the column others, equally weary, did the same.

Dawson's friend Howlett fretted at the delay. "We should keep movin'," he said. "If we lose much more time we won't see the *Newfoundland* this night."

Dawson gestured wearily. "We got *orders* to stop."

Squires growled, "I *told* ye, y' can't go agin' the second hand."

"Second hand or no!" Howlett snapped, "I come through too many hard times fer anyone to tell me what to do."

"Go on then! Nobody's stoppin' ya. . . ."

"Alone? Christ! I'd be a fool to go on alone. Ye know that."

It would, indeed, have been the height of folly. What if he tripped and fell on a hummock, injuring himself, as happened sometimes? What if he fell through the ice? Even in fine weather ice hunters never went anywhere alone.

Again there was talk of the *Greenland*, but Cecil Mouland was too ebullient, dog-tired as he was, to admit the possibility of a disaster.

"'Twill come out all right, ye'll see," he asserted.

His cousin Ralph was less optimistic. "I hope ye're right, Cec, b'y," he said.

"We'll get aboard our ship, Ralph," Cecil promised. "Don't worry."

Pear, with Tuff's help, eventually caught up, and the column moved once more, Jones and his men ranging off to the side, peering through the blizzard, scanning the ice for signs of the disrupted path. But Pear had no sooner started than he began to fall behind again. He got progressively worse, and Tuff at last delegated two men to stay with him, leading him by the arms. He was so ill now as to be all but helpless, and there was no doubt that if the party waited for him they would be out all night. With appalling swiftness the daylight was fading. The thick weather would bring the fall of night at least an hour early.

Tuff, worried by the approaching dusk, called another halt.

"Five or six of the smartest men will go on to the *Newfoundland* as fast as they can fer help," he said. "We'll need a stretcher fer the sick man."

"I'll go," Sidney Jones offered, and started forward with four or five of his watch. Immediately the column moved on with renewed energy, all grimly aware that the remaining moments of daylight were now precious.

Wes Kean, on deck in spite of the storm, noted that the wind kept backing to the east, then veering south and south-east again. He was not worried, though. His men were safely on board the *Stephano* with his father, he felt sure. He had seen them climb aboard, and he knew that the Old Man wouldn't have put them on the ice in this weather. Still, if he had a radio he could make certain. Ah, he was worrying unduly.

Green wrote up the log: *4 p.m. Moderate gale with snow. Wind east-south-east, force 6. Barometer 30.15.* The drop of 25 points since the last entry suggested that the gale would increase in violence, he decided.

Bo'sun Tizzard had now begun to worry about the *Newfoundland*'s crew. But he didn't mention his concern to anyone.

At St. John's the barograph at 4 P.M. registered 28.80, a further drop of 30 tenths in four hours. The city crouched under the howling blizzard; yet the glass was still falling, which meant that the storm centre had not yet passed the city.

# CHAPTER TEN

The *Florizel*, blowing her whistle every few minutes, steamed cautiously south-east. Joe Kean had picked up all the *Stephano*'s men in his vicinity and checked with the ice-masters to see that all members of each party were on board. It was stormy but mild, and he expected it to clear before night.

The *Stephano* was moving his way, but still stopping for pelts. So it was late afternoon before the ships met, and hove-to within hailing distance. The Old Man, never one to waste time, ordered the exchange of crews to start immediately. As they climbed on board the *Florizel*, Joe Kean's six men soon spread the word that the *Newfoundland*'s crew had been left on the ice.

Hearing the rumour, Nathan Kean approached Master Watch Noseworthy. "Are the *Newfoundland*'s men aboard of Father?" he asked.

Noseworthy replied, "They were, sir, but they were put out again soon as they had a mug-up."

Meanwhile, Joe, on the bridge, hailed his father.

"What about the *Newfoundland*'s crew?" he called through cupped hands.

Abram Kean raised his right hand and called back, "Ahl rate!"

Joe Kean accepted this assurance with relief. If the Old Man said they were all right, then of course they were. As the last of his men tumbled over the rail he ordered his ship put about to collect the panned pelts she had left to the north-west.

Joe's query apparently raised some shade of doubt in Captain Abram's mind. He ordered his ship south-east, back to the place where she had panned her first seals.

"We'll steam back to where we picked up Wes's men," he told Yetman. "If any men should happen to be coming t'wards us, we'll be sure to get 'em. We'll sound the whistle."

It was possible, after all, that they might have been panning seals until the storm hit. But considering he had taken them so far to the south, it was likely, even then, that they would head for their own ship. In any case, they would be safe with George Tuff.

Below decks, opinions were unanimous: The men should not have been put on the ice; once there, they should not have been left to find a ship on their own.

Ever since he had got back on board the *Stephano* Mark Sheppard had worked hard, stowing seals, and the occasional pan was still being picked up as they worked south-eastward. The deck was covered with snow and grease, the wind baffling from various quarters. The ice had stretched abroad by now so that you could only work the seals on the lee side. When Mark went below to put on oilskins he heard the discussion about the *Newfoundland*'s crew.

"What's gonna happen to they poor fellers?"

"Where are they, that's what I'd like to know?"

"Is we going to look fer 'em or not?"

Maybe that's why they were heading on a southerly course now, they conjectured, but nobody knew anything for sure, and nobody approached the captain. He was a man who made all his decisions in chilly isolation, and everyone from Yetman down was afraid of him.

"What do *you* think of the *Newfoundland*'s men?" one of them asked Sheppard.

Mark, knowing what it was like on deck, answered, "It's pretty bad now, I'll tell ye. They wouldn't walk anywhere in this."

He thought it over for a minute. "'Twould be well if someone were to pass word to the captain to go an' look for 'em," he suggested.

"That it would. But who?"

There was silence. No one volunteered. But later, after still another stop, when Master watch Garland Gaulton called his men to stow down more pelts, Mark Sheppard approached him.

"It might be better, Skipper," Mark said to Gaulton, "if the ship went lookin' fer the *Newfoundland*'s men, instead of pickin' up swiles. I think every man in the hold would like it better, too."

"So would I, mister," Gaulton replied.

"Why don't ye go to the captain, then, an' see will he look fer 'em?"

At that moment a seaman who had been working in the fore-rigging came down to the deck, and Gaulton turned his attention to him, cutting the conversation short. Mark walked away, and went back to the hold, where the sealers were grumbling furiously at their captain. If he *was* on the way to look for the *Newfoundland*'s men he was taking his dead time about it.

It was five o'clock before Garland Gaulton went to the bridge.

"How'd ye do with the swiles?" the Old Man asked.

Garland told him, then put the question that was worrying everybody except Abram Kean himself. "We heard, sir, that the *Newfoundland*'s crew was aboard us today while we was on the ice. Do ye think they got back to their own ship?"

"I do," the Old Man answered with great authority. "Most decidedly."

There was no room for argument, and Gaulton turned to leave the bridge. It was not his place to question the captain's judgement, or to ask him to go looking for men that he was sure were miles away on their own ship.

But as he was leaving the bridge he heard the Old Man say to the second hand, "Keep the whistle blowing, Fred. We'll steam up to the seal carcasses slowly, and if there's any men on the ice we'll find 'em on our way up."

Blowing her whistle every five minutes, the *Stephano* steamed southward, still gathering pelts on the leeward side and hoisting them aboard. In her holds the sealers fretted uneasily, but did nothing constructive about it.

The common hands were not alone in their worry. Captain William Martin, a master mariner relegated to the role of navigator for the seal hunt, also approached Captain Kean to ask if he was sure that the *Newfoundland*'s men had been able to get on board their ship. Captain Kean replied that they had undoubtedly gotten on board before this, and that he had great faith in their leader, George Tuff.

That was as far as Captain Martin would go. It was not his business to argue about the running of the ship, and he was under orders from the owners not to interfere with Captain Kean's decisions in any way.

The *Newfoundland* had not moved. The wind shrieked through her rigging. Her timbers groaned in the ice. Snow isolated her from the world.

In the hold, with its empty tiers of wooden bunks, her depleted crew huddled around the "bogey." On its flat top a kettle simmered, emitting a wisp of steam with the tang of bitter tea. Stephen Jordan prowling restlessly from one end of the hold to the other, accepted the unspoken sympathy of his companions.

"The cap'n said they got on board the *Stephano*," one volunteered.

"Yah! So 'e said," Jordan muttered, "but I got a feelin' they'm out on the ice, an' me young brother an' two nephews with 'em. I got a feelin' I shoulda stuck by the b'ys."

"I got a feelin' too," another man asserted.

"Why ain't the whistle blowin'? That's what I want to know. Christ! They could be walkin' around in circles out there," Jordan agonized.

"I pities them poor fellers, I do," one murmured, helping himself to a cup of strong tea and thanking his lucky stars he had had sense enough to follow the crowd back to the ship.

Jordan continued his prowling, unable to sit, unable to eat.

Bo'sun Tizzard was also uneasy. Like the others, he had not actually seen the men board the *Stephano*. Ordinarily, when he was on watch duty in a storm he blew the whistle as a matter of course; but he wasn't on watch duty at this time, and thus had no authority to do anything. However, he reasoned, the rest of the officers were with the sealers; there was no officer except himself to take the initiative; *someone* should blow the whistle.

It was late afternoon when he went to the cabin. Green and the chief steward were with Wes Kean.

"It's wonderful starmy, Cap'n," he said, "can't see a hand before your face. Will I blow the whistle?"

"There's not much need for the whistle," Wes decided. "All our men are on board the *Stephano*."

Tizzard looked at the captain with mixed feelings. Even if the men were on another ship, it *was* stormy, and there was always the possibility of *somebody* being astray in the storm. Feeling it was all wrong, he backed through the door.

"You can give it a blow or two if you like," Wes added as an afterthought, just as Tizzard was leaving.

The bo'sun interpreted this literally. He gave the whistle two blows, the limit allowed by the captain, fifteen minutes apart.

After Tizzard had left, Wes remarked, to no one in particular, "God knows who might be on the ice." The way floes wheeled in a storm he knew it was possible that men from *any* ship might be within earshot of the *Newfoundland*'s signal. But although he knew this, he did not order the whistle to continue sounding.

On the ice Tuff was having a difficult time. Jones and his handful of men were struggling to hurry ahead, but it was impossible to make any speed. They couldn't see, and the swirling snow confused their sense of direction. More and more often, they were off the path. But now there was desperation, and from this they drew strength.

Cecil Mouland felt that it was all a little unreal, a nightmare that would vanish at any moment. The sense of nightmare actually seemed to remove him from the real world of danger; he seemed not to be on the ice, but somewhere else. Voices came to him in snatches, rising in consternation or fear.

"Jaysus!"

"Give us a hand, will ya?"

"Oh, my God!"

"We'm gonna die, fellers." A voice rose somewhere near. "We ain't never gonna see our families again."

Cecil heard it numbly. None of it was really happening.

A blackened pinnacle rising on a swell, a smear of blood left by one of the pelts the men had towed back to the ship that day, a flag-pole leaning crazily out of a drift, all in turn gave them renewed hope.

Under their weight small pans dipped, and many legs felt the ominous trickle of icy sea water through leather boots. Cecil's young friend Art Mouland did not get off so easily; he fell right in to the waist. His cry of fright roused Cecil from his trance, and he and another man hauled Art up on an ice pan. The boy was soaked to the skin. Shivering with cold and shock he staggered a few steps and then gradually fell behind. Cecil, sunk again in a world of reeling fantasy, did not realize until later that Art was missing. He was never seen again.

Daylight was now tinged with premature dusk, and they knew they were still far from their ship. Dawson, Squires, and Jones had broken trail all the way and were so exhausted they could barely lift their feet. Tuff would not delegate anyone else to lead, and no one would go against Tuff's wishes.

Howlett, directly behind the lead men, fumed with impatience: "Dammit! We're crawlin'!"

William Pear, at the end of the column and on the verge of collapse, was being almost carried from pan to pan. His glasses were gone, and he stared blindly into the storm.

At last Tuff called another halt and lugged Pear forward into the midst of the men.

"We've got a sick man here," he said, "and he's holdin' us back. Now if there's two men on the ice tonight I'm goin' to be one of 'em, but I'm callin' fer volunteers to stay with us—two volunteers. Then the rest of ye strike out fer the ship as fast as you can."

Who would volunteer? Twenty-six-year-old Stanley Andrews stepped forward with another man whose name was never recorded.

"Good enough," said Tuff. "Now the rest of you *hurry!*"

They struggled wearily into the storm and Tuff turned to Pear.

"Now then, me son, ye'll have to cheer up and do the best ye can. Are ye hungry?"

"Yes, sir," Pear croaked.

Tuff had two cakes of hard tack and a can of sardines. "What'll ye have?" Pear indicated the sardines, and Tuff opened the tin and passed it to him. The sick man ate the small fish, the oil trickling down his chin.

"How was that?" Tuff asked. "Ye feel better?"

"Much better, sir."

"Can ye go on now?"

"Yes, sir. I can walk. But I can't see much."

Andrews and the other sealer took him by the arms. "Come on, ol' man," they encouraged.

The wind gusted heavily, increasing in force. Their faces ached from it. The air was growing cold, they noticed. Snow, not sticky any more, was now drifting freely, obscuring the trail.

At this point the 132 men on the ice were divided into three groups: the small group led by Jones, scouting the trail and trying to reach the ship for help; the main group led by Dawson; the little party of four led by Tuff. The groups ahead were still managing to find poles or other traces of the trail from time to time.

Suddenly, those up front were electrified by the sound of a ship's whistle. Borne with the wind it came to them plainly.

"It's our whistle! It's the *Newfoundland*'s whistle!" Richard McCarthy shouted joyously.

They were saved!

Instantly, weariness departed. New life from somewhere surged into their legs. They pressed forward.

Master Watches Jones, Dawson, and Mouland all heard the whistle from their various stations on the ice. To Jones it had sounded very close indeed. Checking his pocket watch he found it was 4:30.

"Shout, men!" he ordered. "Shout as loud as ye can! See if they can hear us!"

All cupped their hands and hollered together into the storm, "Hoy-y-y-y! *Newfoundland!*"

Only the wail of the wind came back to them.

"Where did the whistle come from?" one asked uncertainly.

"The sou'east, b'y."

"We're wastin' our strength. The wind blows our v'ices away from the ship."

"They *might* have heard us," someone said hopefully.

"Depends on how far away she is."

They shouted again, not so certain now of the direction from which the whistle had come.

"It *gotta* be the sou'east. That's where the *Newfoundland* is."

They slogged on through snow that hugged their knees, listening, straining their ears, expecting every minute to see the black shape of the ship looming through the storm. Fifteen minutes later the whistle blew again. It did not seem any louder than before.

"Hear that?"

"Did it come from the sou'east?"

"Yeah, I guess it gotta be."

"Don't stand around jawin'," Dawson growled. "Get movin'."

"Which way, Skipper?"

"George said to keep the wind on yer left cheek. That's what we'll do."

They continued, not certain of anything any more. They had lost the trail.

Master Watch Arthur Mouland now bitterly regretted having forgotten his compass that morning. With a compass, even now, he was sure he could find the *Newfoundland*, but apparently none of the men in his watch had a compass, and lord knew where the other master watches were. Once before, sealing on the *Falcon* under Captain Job Kean he had been caught on the ice like this in a storm, but at the first blast of the ship's whistle he had taken a compass bearing, and within a short time was on the *Falcon*'s deck. Now to be so near . . . and without a compass . . .

Precious time was lost tracking back and forth trying to find the lost trail. At last someone saw a wooden pole leaning out of a snowbank. It encouraged them to go on. Each moment they expected to hear the whistle again, to see their ship looming out of the snow. They *had* to come upon her any minute. . . .

The minutes passed. The wind grew higher. The path, if there *was* any path, could no longer be seen. They listened . . . and listened . . . and the whistle did not sound again.

Tired as he was, Dawson tried to encourage them.

"She can't be far," he said. "That whistle couldn't have come from more'n a mile away."

Presently they stumbled upon a heap of rubbish: broken stabber poles, garbage, cinders drawn from her furnaces, the trash that a ship throws out each day. *They were almost there.*

"She's close by!" Howlett yelled. "She's gotta be around here some place!"

But the whistle did not sound, and they stumbled forward again, facing the wind.

They passed more rubbish and, straining their ears, trudged forward, grimly silent. There had to be *some* sound from the ship!

Suddenly they were in a trackless waste. All signs of the path were gone, obliterated by the snow, or simply lost. Jones and his men shouted to Dawson that the path was lost, and Dawson and his men tracked back and forth, searching vainly for the signs that had guided them thus far. They found none.

Sidney Jones was discouraged. "We can't find the track, fellers. I think we'd better start hollerin' again. Maybe we'm near enough now for someone on the *Newfoundland* to hear us."

Cupping mittened hands around their mouths, they shouted hoarsley, "Hoy-y-y-y!"

Meanwhile Tuff and his party had not heard the whistle at all. They had been far behind, following the others' tracks. They had coaxed the sick man along at a snail's pace, and now they arrived where they could hear the others shouting.

"You hear that, men? They've found the *Newfoundland*!" Tuff roared.

Sure that they were shouting to let him know they had found the ship, he shouted back, "We're coming-g-g-g!" Stanley Andrews and the other sealer joined him, their voices carrying raggedly against the wind, "Hoy-y-y-y!"

Jones, hearing the shouts of men back along the track, hastily gathered his party. "They found her! They found the *Newfoundland*!" he said.

"I *knowed* we passed her," one observed.

"What odds, we're getting aboard, that's the main thing." They hurried back along their track, suddenly tired no more . . . until they came upon the four stragglers.

Tuff yelled, "Did ye see the steamer?"

Jones called, "No! Did you? Someone was shoutin'. . . ."

It was a bitter disappointment—shattering. If *only* her whistle would sound again!

Now Dawson and his men loomed out of the snow, confirming the fact that no trace of the path could be found. Unable to keep on their feet another minute, Dawson and Jones dropped where they stood. Several others also sank down to the ice, resting.

Knee-deep in snow drifts, the men closed around Tuff. One voiced an opinion: "Skipper, I think we'm gone past our ship." Another suggested that the wind had veered. "We'm goin' round in circles, that's what."

Tuff simply said, flatly, "We're lost, men."

Darkness was settling swiftly. The swells were now noticeably steeper, a fact that made them suspect they were near the edge of the ice-field, for "the ice flattens out the sea."

Tuff turned to the nearest sealer: "Take charge of the sick man."

So John Howlett found himself in charge of Pear, a man he thought had no business on the ice at all.

"Gather round," Tuff ordered. "It looks like a night on the ice."

There was a restless stir among the crowd, and Tuff exhorted: "There's nothing for us to do but put up with it, like men."

Just then, from beyond the fringe of the party, there came a shout: "I've found it! I found the path!"

There were, indeed, signs, and they examined them with renewed hope: cinders, broken stabber poles, rubbish—was it the same they had passed before? They didn't think so.

"Where is she?"

"She's around here somewhere."

She *had* to be. *Why* didn't she sound her whistle?

They had gone only some three or four hundred yards when they were again in a trackless waste. The last faint hint of daylight was fading. There could be no more tracking for the path.

"This is where we stop for the night," Tuff decided.

They all gathered around him in a tight, anxious cluster.

"Stand back! Spread out!" he ordered. "We could sink this pan if a hundred an' more of us crowd onto it!" Then he called, "Master Watches!"

Dawson, Mouland, Bungay, and Jones came forward.

"Each of you will take your watch and separate," he said. "Pick a large ice pan and build a shelter—make it as comfortable as you can."

A "shelter" meant a wall. The men from the *Greenland*, too, had built shelters.

The two younger master watches, Jones and Bungay, hung back.

"Will you come with me in my watch, Mr. Tuff?" Jones asked.

"I was gonna ask you the same thing, Skipper George," Bungay said.

They all knew that Tuff had been through the terrible *Greenland* disaster, and would have an idea what you must do to keep alive. Tuff weighed matters, and decided to go with the youngest officer, Bungay. Sidney Jones, reeling with exhaustion, would have to cope on his own.

Just before the fall of night, Wes Kean had sent for Tizzard.

"Bo'sun," he said, "pick four men for watch duty. All the master watches are gone, so in the mornin' ye'll have to go to the barrel to scun her through the ice."

Tizzard accepted the orders with good grace. His duties were on deck, but since all other officers were gone, someone had to take over. He went to the holds to pick his men for deck watch, and they came crowding around him.

"Why isn't the whistle blowin'?" Jordan demanded.

Tizzard could feel himself growing defensive: "Because the cap'n said I could give it a blow or two, and that's what I done."

"A blow or two's no bloody good to a bunch of men lost in a starm!" Jordan exclaimed.

Tizzard said doggedly, "The cap'n is certain his men are aboard the *Stephano*. He seen 'em go on board hisself."

"Yah! But I got me doubts about that!" Jordan said.

They all had their doubts, and this did nothing to ease Tizzard's mind. But he had no authority to go on blowing the whistle. He felt that his orders had been clear: a blow or two.

At supper Wes Kean ate heartily, envisioning pelts piled high on pans and waiting for them tomorrow. Now if this gale, with the swell it was kicking up, would just loosen the ice enough to get the *Newfoundland* a mile or two to the westward, he'd be in the clear. . . . Outside the wind moaned and the rigging complained. It was a damn dirty night. The wind seemed to be rising, too.

"At least our men are all right," Wes said to Green, the only man who shared his table that night. "They're on the *Stephano* and Father will look after them. They'll have a chance to exchange 'cuffers' with the men on the *Stephano*."

Supper finished, he put on his sealskin cap and coat and went to the bridge. Wind and snow made the night completely blind.

He hurried below to look at the barometer on the wall just outside his private cabin.

"Fair," it proclaimed.

Wes had an almost superstitious belief in the barometer. To see it pointing to "Fair" in a raging blizzard annoyed him.

"What's all this fuss about?" he said to Green. "The glass don't show fer it!"

It was impossible, Green knew, for the pressure to be what the glass said it was, in the middle of a storm like this. It should have been sent to Roper's to be checked and set before leaving St. John's. It hadn't been set for years, and nobody knew how inaccurate it was.


On board the *Florizel* Captain Joe Kean was worried. His younger brother Nathan had relayed to him the information that the *Newfoundland*'s men had been put back on the ice, Nathan didn't know just where. The thought nagged him as the weather worsened. He hoped his father had gone back to pick them up after all his own men were on board. Was that what he meant when he waved and said, "Ahl rate?" He worried about it all through supper.

Breaking in on his thoughts, the steward reported that they were getting low on drinking water.

"We'll get some fresh ice tonight," Joe promised, and went back to his worries.

The meal over, he went to the bridge. The wind was becoming more violent, and backing towards the north. That meant the worst was yet to come. It would be blowing a gale and a half from the north-west before it was finished, he judged. If the *Newfoundland*'s men were on the ice, then they were in terrible trouble. Still, his father had said they were all right, and one didn't question the Old Man in matters of that kind. Blast it! If Wes had a wireless there'd be none of this worry!

A few minutes before seven he ordered the ship to stop, and a party of men to collect fresh-water ice from the floes. Compacted snow or frozen rain-water would do, but the best for drinking was the lovely blue-green glacial ice from the Arctic. Luckily there was plenty of Arctic ice around.

Finally, unable to stand the worry any longer, Joe went to the wireless shack to dictate an unofficial message to his father. Patrick Barkley scribbled the note: "Have you the *Newfoundland*'s men on board?" it read.

Steaming along in a leisurely way on a south-south-east bearing, her whistle blowing intermittently, the *Stephano* continued to pick up an occasional pan of seals, though it was too stormy for Second Hand Yetman to see much beyond the ship, and he was uncertain of their exact position. The ice was tightening, and the going getting difficult, when, around six o'clock, a flag loomed off the port bow in heavy ice. The Old Man ordered his ship close enough to see that it was a *Florizel* flag, and satisfied himself that it was the flag close to the spot where he had picked up the *Newfoundland*'s crew that morning. Now he knew where he was, and here he would remain, "snuggled up" to the heavy ice. If the *Newfoundland*'s men *were* returning to the *Stephano* they could do it either by following the trail of dead carcasses, or by skirting the edge of the big ice. Either way, they could hardly miss his ship. Satisfied that he had done his best, Abram Kean burned down for the night, leaving orders with Yetman to keep the whistle blowing at intervals.

Though the Old Man was now satisfied he knew exactly where he was, Yetman, who had scunned the ship through the ice all the way, calculated her in a different position, at least a mile to a mile and a half farther south than Captain Kean believed. In his estimation they were now down to the bulge of the big ice, or even a bit southward of it, close to the place where they had dropped the *Newfoundland*'s men. They did not consult each other about this. They had no reason to do so.

At 7:34 P.M. Joe's message was delivered to the Old Man: "Have you the *Newfoundland*'s men on board?"

At 8 P.M. the Old Man came to the conclusion that there was no one on the ice within range of his ship and ordered the whistle stopped.

At 8:19 he sent his reply to Joe: "Carried *Newfoundland*'s crew within three miles ship before noon, have no doubt they are aboard their own ship."

The men on the ice were lost, unutterably weary, their reserves of strength low after hours of rough travel. Wet feet and damp clothes added to their misery. The wind whistled through the night, tearing at them. A few voices gloomed: "We'm never gonna see home again." And who could honestly deny the danger? Weren't they already on their last legs through fatigue?

"We'm gonna die." The whisper went here and there throughout the crowd.

Cecil Mouland said to his cousin Ralph: "*I'm* not gonna die." In his mind's eye he could see Jessie's serious young face, and the faces of half a dozen other young men who had an eye on her. No sir, none of them fellers were going to get Jessie!" "I don't know about you fellers, but *I'm* not gonna die," he said grimly.

Most of them took it gamely enough, and answered the call as Dawson, Mouland, and Bungay gave orders to the men of their watches. Jones's watch hung around waiting for orders, but he gave none, so they distributed themselves among the other watches, mostly those of Dawson and Mouland. Now they formed three groups on three pans within hailing distance of one another. Jones himself went to Dawson's pan. Howlett, with William Pear in tow, went with Dawson, whom he had been with all day. Benjamin Piercey attached himself to Mouland's watch since that was where most of the New Perlican men were.

A check proved that the pans offered little protection in the form of pinnacles or rafters under which they could take shelter, but the edges were rough and hummocky, with many loose cakes of ice piled up around them. Beyond their floes, lesser pans rose and fell steeply, confirming their fear that they were dangerously close to the edge of the ice-field. Pans had been known to scatter, the men on them driven off to sea. . . .

"All hands set to and build shelters," was the order.

To build even simple shelters was a monumental chore for the exhausted men. It meant chopping at the ice hummocks with their gaffs until they had enough loose blocks of ice to build a crude wall, then plastering it with snow until it would serve as a wind break. They simply didn't have the strength.

In Arthur Mouland's watch only a handful of men made half-hearted attempts to find and bring ice blocks to the place he indicated, and his voice crackled with annoyance.

"*All* hands will bring ice to build a gaze," he snapped. And since many still stood around, shivering and drooping, he said brusquely, "I don't mean one or two hands build a gaze, *I mean all of you*. Get busy."

The "gaze" took its name from its use in hunting, but it would serve a different end tonight. Since the chill factor of the wind might be equal to 30 or 40 degrees of temperature, the gaze might well mean the difference between life and death.

Mouland drove them on relentlessly as they dragged the ice into place with their weary limbs, stabbing with their gaffs, ready at every move to fall on their faces. After a long time they had a wall, thirty feet long, running across the pan so as to break the wind from the east-south-east. They had built near enough to the edge to use the hummocky ice as part of the wall, and Mouland had made them keep at it until it was a foot higher than their heads. All the holes were liberally plastered with wet snow. Soon they were protected from everything except the drift that broke over the top and sifted softly down upon them.

But Mouland still was not satisfied.

"All right," he said. "Now I want the ends turned in."

They grumbled that it was good enough, but he drove them on. They plodded back and forth, bringing more ice, packing more snow, until they had lost all feeling in their arms and all sense of time—it was a labour that would never end. But at last the two wings were built, and he was satisfied.

"If the wind shifts we'll *need* them ends," he said.

They huddled in the shelter while the wind keened over their heads. Huddled with them were some men from Sidney Jones's watch, men who had taken no part in the building and who, Mouland thought, were dangerously overcrowding the plan.

Mouland ordered them off. "Go find your own master watch," he said. "You're not stayin' with us."

His voice brooked no argument, and the leaderless men slunk away, all except Benjamin Piercey. "Can I stay, Mr. Mouland?"

"You're not in my watch."

"No, sir, but I'm from New Perlican, and all the New Perlican men are with you. They're my chums. I don't know them other fellers." While Mouland considered this, Piercey added, "They're all gone now, sir, and it's too dark and dangerous for a man to go wanderin' around the ice alone."

"Stay then," Mouland agreed. He did not like ordering men out of his shelter, but it was the men of his watch he had set himself to save.

On his pan, Dawson ordered: "Stick yer gaffs in the snow, men. Line 'em up against the wind. . . . Now, get blocks of ice an' lay 'em along the gaffs."

They did so, slowly, clumsily, their bodies aching with weariness. Jones, who had hovered around Dawson, now melted into the crowd and disappeared. His men hung around the fringes of Dawson's watch. They did not offer to help build the shelter. Noting this, Dawson snapped, "What are *ye* standin' around fer? Get to work."

Some of them did, but others refused to budge. "We don't take orders from you, Tom Dawson."

"If ye stay on this pan ye do," Dawson threatened, but he was too physically exhausted to make good any kind of threat, and most of them knew it.

His wall grew slowly, extending across the floe. At last it was shoulder-high, and they stopped.

"That's not high enough, men, get on with it," he ordered.

"Skipper, we can't lift our arms no higher; we got no strength left," they protested.

"Besides, it's mild, Skipper Tom; it's gonna turn to rain," another said.

Dawson knew just how they felt, and he, too, expected it to rain and then clear off.

"It should be higher," he said, "but I guess it'll do."

Already some of his men were crouching beneath the wall, shredding their tow ropes, cutting shavings from their gaff stems. A match flared in cupped hands, and in a few minutes flames were licking upwards, crackling around the greasy wood as gaff handles and flagpoles were sacrificed. Three men removed their boots and dried their wet socks. Now, if only they had a seal or two. They thought longingly of the panned seals they had left, several hours back, under the *Stephano*'s flag. They got out their hard tack, and began chewing it.

On Bungay's pan the situation was much the same. The men had laboured to erect a shelter, but had balked at building it higher than arm level: "Skipper we'm tired."

Tuff did not insist, so Bungay didn't.

In the shelter of the ice walls little fires flickered and glowed as the men dug into their meagre rations—hard tack for most, rolled oats and raisins for a few, here and there a tin of molasses mixed with Radway's Ready Relief. They had no regular utensils, but here and there a tin, containing snow, was held over a fire to be heated. Hot water mixed with Radway's really warmed your insides.

(1)  A Newfoundland outport around 1914, typical of the ones from which the sealers flocked to join the fleet at St. John's.

(2)  The port of St. John's shortly after that date.

(3) When ice stopped a sealing ship from getting out of harbour the crew had to drag her through. Here, with "everybody on the line," the ill-fated *Southern Cross* tries to get out of St. John's Harbour.

(4) (*Below*) Tall floating icebergs were a constant menace to the sealing ships.

(5) (*Bottom*) The object of the search—seals on the ice. These seals are hoods, more dangerous than the commoner harp seals. Close by are several blow holes.

(6)(7) Two sealers ready for the ice. Not all sealers were uniformly warmly dressed, and goggles to protect their eyes from the glare of the ice were not commonly worn. Note the rough planking laid down to protect the decks from the sealers' hobnailed boots.

(8) A blood-stained sealer ready to return to the ice, complete with tow rope, gaff, and flag-pole.

(9) The departure of the sealing fleet was a major event of the year in St. John's.

(10)  The steel ice-breakers had little trouble steaming through small loose ice.

(11)  "Swiles!" At that cry the hunters were always eager to go overboard on the ice.

(12)(13)  When they received the order "Over the side, me b'ys!" the sealers would pour over the ship's side on the ice, pausing there to arrange their burden for the long walk to the seals.

(14)(15)   Soon the ice-field would be alive with black files of men snaking towards the nearest patch of seals. Often the going was far from smooth.

(16)(17)  Loose pans of ice were a constant hazard and sealers had to "coppy" across them. Less agile sealers could get their feet wet, which was a serious matter on the ice-field.

(18)  Young men at the
ice for the first time had
to nerve themselves to
make the first kill.

(19)(20)  "Sculping" seals took little time. When the pelts were ready they were dragged to the nearest collecting pan or back to the ship.

(21) In ideal conditions sealers drag their catch back to their ship across clear, flat ice.

(22)(23) Here, in loose ice, the hides are winched aboard.

(24) An expert flensing a hide—separating the fat—with a sculping knife.

(25) The results of a successful voyage; pelts begin to pile up as they are dumped ashore at St. John's.

(25A)(25B)  Captain Abram Kean. "Old Man" Kean was the most famous and most successful sealing captain of all time, and everyone went in awe of him. In 1914 he was skipper of the *Stephano* at the ice.

(26) One of the vessels involved in the 1914 tragedy, the *Florizel*.

(27) The *Florizel's* skipper, Captain Joseph Kean, eldest son of the "Old Man."

(29) The *Newfoundland* below an inset of her young skipper, Captain Westbury Kean, another of Abram Kean's sons.

(28) The wooden *Newfoundland* built forty-two years before the disaster. She was one of the few ships without wireless in 1914.

(30) George Tuff, second hand of the *Newfoundland*, was the officer in charge of the men lost on the ice.

(31) Among the men was young Cecil Mouland, determined to live to marry his sweetheart, Jessie.

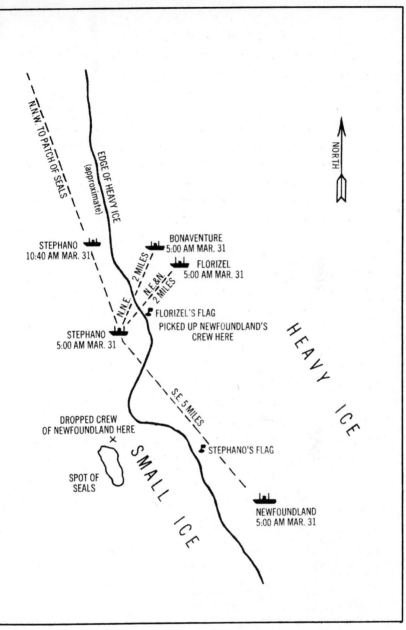

(32)    Map of the disaster area.

(33)   Captain Robert Randell and the rescue ship *Bellaventure*.

(34)   Winding around the heavy rafters of Arctic ice, crewmen of the *Bellaventure* carry stretchers to bring back the dead and the near dead. The smoke from the *Bellaventure* shows at the top left of the picture.

(35)   (*Top right*)   The *Bellaventure*'s crew bring in the dead on stretchers and in their arms. They found many of the dead frozen to the ice. In the background a flag, planted to bring rescuers to the disaster, still flutters forlornly. Beyond that, the *Stephano* steams about searching for other survivors.

(36)   (*Middle right*)   From a stretcher a frozen arm points to the sky as the dead sealers are brought to the rescue ship.

(37)   (*Bottom right*)   From the *Bellaventure* men watch in horror as the frozen bodies are carried towards the ship. At the top right of the picture is the pitiful shelter built by Arthur Mouland's men, and survivors still huddle behind its walls.

(38)  Some survivors were able to walk, with assistance. Here one is helped aboard the *Bellaventure* after two days and two nights on the ice.

(39)  As they are brought aboard the *Bellaventure* the dead are laid on the forehatch in the well of the ship.

(40)  Stacked like cordwood, three deep, the seventy-seven frozen bodies of the *Newfoundland*'s crew lie on the forehatch of the *Bellaventure*.

(41)   With her flag at half-mast, the *Bellaventure* arrives in the port of St. John's on Saturday, April 4, 1914, bearing a grim cargo. Behind the *Bellaventure* is historic Signal Hill.

(42)   Citizens of St. John's crowd Harvey's waterfront premises to await the arrival of the *Bellaventure*. The Red Ensign flies at half-mast.

(43)   An estimated ten thousand persons waited all day for a glimpse of the *Bellaventure* and the survivors. They were remarkably silent and solemn, according to the newspaper reports.

(44)   A tarpaulin covers the frozen sealers while preparations are made to remove the bodies.

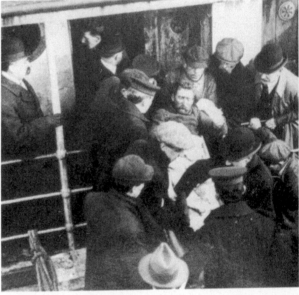

(45)   Ralph Mouland, Cecil Mouland's cousin, shows the strain of his ordeal as he is lifted carefully over the side. He survived, but lost both of his feet.

(46)   Master Watch Thomas Dawson anxiously favours his frost-bitten hands as he is lifted over the railing. Dawson lost both feet. The man wearing the bowler hat (top left) is the Acting Premier, the Honourable John R. Bennett.

(47)   (*Left*) Chairs placed together and covered with sheets form receptacles for the bodies of the dead sealers until they are thawed, identified, and prepared for coffining.

(48)  Two young survivors in hospital. On the right is Hedley Payne and on the left is Cecil Tiller.

(49)  Cecil Mouland did survive to marry his sweetheart, Jessie. This photograph was taken fifty years after the disaster.

# CHAPTER ELEVEN

Aboard the *Stephano*, the atmosphere was one of anxiety and anger. Rumours were flying about the ship that the glass was "bottom up." This meant that the wind would soon chop from the north and west with hard frost, and that would be rough for any man on the ice that night. And the *Newfoundland's* men were out there. Of that every sealer was dead certain.

Sam Horwood, the master of his own ship and of a fishing crew, a man used to responsibility, felt compelled to forsake the comparative warmth of the hold and go on deck to see if the weather was improving at all. It wasn't. Raw winds backing northward and a solid wall of snow verified his worst fears. He prowled aft, met a deck hand and stopped to chat, voicing the anxiety of the crew below deck. But the deck hand was an ordinary sealer like himself, and Horwood felt the need to express his anxiety to men of authority. Someone had to pass the word along, so he went forward to the saloon and found the wheelsman, Samuel Kean. Ah! he thought, here was the Old Man's own brother; this was one sure way to get word to the captain.

Skipper Sam Horwood eased himself into a chair beside "Uncle" Sam Kean and hauled out his old pipe. Horwood was a simple, blunt, and forceful man, and he didn't believe in beating about the bush. "If the *Newfoundland's* crew is on the ice tonight, Uncle Sam, what d' ye think of it?" he asked directly.

Sam Kean, after due deliberation, replied, "If they'm on the ice they have a turrible dirty night." Then he added thoughtfully,

"If they stopped to kill swiles, I don't see how they could get on board."

Horwood nodded, pointing the stem of his pipe at Kean, "To my mind, sir, even if the *didn't* stop to kill swiles, they didn't get on board. There's a rumour about the ship that the glass is bottom up, and if that's the case, we're sure to have th' wind from the narth and west and *freezin'*, and them men will surely perish on the ice."

Sam Kean thought it over and agreed. "I'm afraid so." But after a moment he changed the subject. "What's yer name, me son, and where do ye belong to?" he asked.

"Me name is Sam Horwood, of Carbonear, sir, master of a Labrador schooner. Ye can depend on it, Uncle Sam, it's goin' to be a bad job. Them men will perish on the ice, mark my words!"

Sam Kean neither agreed nor disagreed, and Horwood, sure now that their fears for the *Newfoundland*'s men would reach the captain's ears through his brother, wished him a "good night" and returned to the hold. It was as good as speaking to the captain himself, he felt.

But what Horwood didn't know was that Sam Kean, too, was afraid of the Old Man. They were *all* afraid of him. So although the men below deck continued to mutter amongst themselves, none had the courage to go to the bridge. The officers spoke cautiously to one another about the *Newfoundland*'s men, but none suggested to the captain that he should go look for them. Who would dare make a suggestion like that to the Old Man? Amongst themselves they professed confidence in Tuff, but still believed that the sealers could easily be out on the ice—and if they were, they were going to have a damn hard time of it.

On the *Florizel* Captain Joe Kean had been reassured when he read his father's wire, "Carried *Newfoundland*'s crew within three miles of ship before noon, have no doubt they are aboard their own ship." So that was what his father meant when he said, "Ahl rate!" What Joe did not know was that his father had sent them off to the south-west hunting seals, not south-east to their ship.

He looked at the message, picturing the men *three miles from their ship*, and that first flood of relief receded. A full-scale blizzard was raging, there had been no let-up at all, and Wes's men had been *three miles* from their ship when put on the ice at the onset of the storm. Could they be sure of finding their way to their ship in a blizzard?

Joe could not shake his uneasiness. Thoughts of a second *Greenland* disaster plagued him, and recalling that one of his officers knew about that disaster in great detail, he sought him out. When he found him, Master Watch John Roberts was in the cabin, yarning with friends. Joe joined them, trying to seem casual, and the steward placed a mug of hot tea before him. Presently, unable to conceal his worry, he said, "I wonder if Wes's men got aboard the *Newfoundland*?"

"Tuff's a good man, he knows what's what," Roberts said.

Do you think they got back, John?" Joe was pressing, anxious for an honest answer, even if it was an unwelcome one. Roberts' seamed, wind-burned face was thoughtful. "They *could've* made it, there was plenty time. But the starm . . ." He shook his head regretfully.

"Yah!" Joe muttered softly. Then he asked, "Is this starm anything like the one that caught the *Greenland*?"

Here John Roberts could reassure him. "No, *sir*! That were a bitter cold starm, that were. Nothin' like this one; this is a mild starm, Cap'n. It's gonna turn to rain pretty soon, so even if Cap'n Wes's men *are* out, they'll come through ahl rate."

It was small comfort, and it only slightly assuaged Joe's uneasiness. He gulped his tea and went back to the bridge.

Damn! If only Wes had wireless.

The ice walls gave the lost sealers only partial shelter. Although it hardly seemed possible, the weather was getting worse. The wind backed from the east to the north and back to the east again, but kept backing farther northward, whistling across the ice-field to lash at the men with the stinging rawness that made their flesh ache. The wet snow clung to their clothes, their hair, their eyebrows, their beards; it trickled icily down their necks. Cecil Mouland thought longingly of the oilskins back in his bunk. If he'd brought 'em along, they would not only keep out the wet snow, but protect him from the wind, too.

Wet, cold, and miserable as they were, the prolonged mildness still convinced them that the weather wouldn't get any worse. They clustered around flickering fires made from their poles, trying to magically draw a little warmth from them. When some of Jones's men, who had done nothing to assist in the building of the shelter, pushed themselves forward to share what little warmth the fires gave, there were howls of indignation. "Get the hell outa here, you . . .!"

But despite their howls and even kicks, the interlopers doggedly remained.

John Howlett had taken great pains to light a fire and nurse it with shavings from his gaff stem. Now, with contributions from other sealers, he had a fine fire going, generating warmth and cheer in the blackness. To this fire Jones's men also crowded, edging away sealers who stretched chilled hands for warmth. There were indignant mutterings from Dawson's men, and a small amount of shoving, but most of their energies had gone into the building of the shelter; they had nothing left over to enable them to assert their rightful places at the fire.

Howlett put an end to it. "You bloody well want a fire, you bloody well build a fire," he yelled, and kicked the blazing sticks to the four winds. They sputtered, smoked, and died.

At this point they made a disconcerting discovery. Those who had been closest to the fire now found the cold more chilling then before; it was as if the heat had "opened their pores" and allowed the wind to burrow in through their skin. They had been numb before, but now their very bones felt naked. They could not stand much more of this, they told one another through chattering teeth; and thereafter they kept a respectable distance from other fires.

Still, some did not heed the wisdom of the few, and snatched the comfort of a blazing fire, happily roasting hands and faces, ignoring the warnings of others not to get too close or stay too long.

"Don't burn all yer gaffs," Dawson warned. "Ye'll need'em to get back to the ship."

Gradually the hard-won fuel ran out and the fires dwindled. One by one they went out. The wind and the cold and the all-enveloping darkness returned.

*Newfoundland log;*
*10 p.m. Strong gale and drifting snow. Ship burned down. Wind force 6.*

It was nearing midnight when the warm air generating all the fury of the storm finally condensed its moisture, and torrential rain replaced the wet snow. Down it came, a cold cloudburst, soaking them to the skin.

The men huddled close to give each other protection and warmth. The two shoulder-high walls couldn't keep them even partially dry. Only those in Arthur Mouland's watch had any real shelter. Their wall was snug and tight. The rain beat against it but could find no loophole. When the wind backed to the north, they crowded to the north corner, which gave them some protection. But beneath their feet the snow turned to slush that soaked through their boots. If they had felt cold and miserable before, they were indescribably wretched now, some of them too wretched to care about living. But so far only one man was missing, and in the rain at least they would not freeze to death.

There was a stir in the crowd. "Get a move on, fellers. Can't stand around. Gotta exercise and kape warm."

There was pushing and prodding as they got on the move, shuffling round and round, so weary they barely realized they were moving, so exhausted that each foot seemed to weigh a ton.

William Pear was too ill to move about. He was not a sea-man. He did not have the stamina of his hardier companions, nor did anyone else at this stage have the stamina to haul a sick man around. They helped him until they could help no more, then they left him alone. Pear sprawled on the ice.

Now they were all soaked to the skin. But the old hands knew that as long as the rain kept up, they were safe. But if it started to freeze . . . They squinted miserably up into the rain, and prayed that it would continue.

For more than an hour the rain beat down in a deluge. Then the storm moved eastward into the Atlantic. Icy air from the north rushed in behind it. Without a lull or a warning, the wind chopped around to the north-north-east, the temperature dropped rapidly to 16 above zero, and the rain froze into pellets of sleet.

The wind chill factor now created conditions equivalent to 20 degrees below zero. Men, wet through, crouched on the ice, had little hope.

About twenty miles north of the *Newfoundland*, the *Nascopie*, all by herself, was burned down snugly. Coaker had written:

*"The early morning was clear at 10 a.m. indications of weather observable. At noon looked as if we would have snow storm, weather mild. At 1 p.m. snow thick, lost sight of men on ice near ship; snow cleared a little and all men taken on board. Captain kept men close to ship all morning. Snowing and blowing bitterly all evening. At nightfall the wind was blowing a gale from the north with snow. Real wintry night. Our men all on board at 1 p.m. when weather came on, considerable swell all day. A stowaway on board ill with mumps and is confined to hospital."*

"Real wintry night." On the ice the men were transfixed as the bitter, snow-laden wind, screaming from the north, quickly turned their sodden clothing to ice. An east wind was one thing, a north wind was quite another. Within moments, ice was clinging to their faces.

"Lard Jaysus!" muttered one.

"I knowed it," Jesse Collins said without any satisfaction. "I tell you, the *Greenland* disaster won't be nothin' to this one."

"Whadda we do, Jesse?" a fledgling sealer asked the older man.

"We *move*, tha's what we do." He stamped his feet. "We move and kape movin', we don't stop fer a minute. Gotta kape warm; kape the blood movin' so it won't freeze in yer veins."

Some followed his example, others stood around as though they were rooted to the ice. Jesse, a vigorous man, walked among them, pushing, prodding: "Move," he ordered roughly.

The ice shelters had given some protection from the east wind, but the sudden shift had left all except Mouland's men exposed to the frosty north wind and driving snow. Since they had built the walls on the edges of their pans, they could not seek shelter on the lee side.

The men of Jones's watch, congregating with Dawson's men, had grossly overcrowded his pan, leaving little space for exercise. Their wall was useless so they devised their own method of protection by standing four deep with their backs to the wind, the men on the windward side running to leeward to take their place at the front until they had worked back to the windward again.

Here and there, from the three different groups, a few voices rose bravely in song. Soon others joined in. But the bitter wind from Labrador buffeted their ill-clad bodies, and snatched their voices, dispersing them raggedly into the night. Others danced lively jigs to halt the freezing numbness creeping insidiously through their limbs. The huskiest sky-larked and even wrestled with each other.

But there were many who by now were too ill with cold and exhaustion to do more than creep feebly about. They lay on the ice to rest.

"*Move*! Kape moving!" was the order, as those with more vitality forced them back to their feet, trying to shock life into them, to make them walk. But Tom Jordan, brother of Stephen, wandered too near the edge of the pan and, unable to distinguish the slush from the solid ice, fell through. His cry of fright brought two men who hauled him back to the floe. There, trembling with shock, he collapsed and died. He was the first man in Dawson's watch to die.

Ice crusted their clothing, their eyebrows and lashes, even the stubble that bearded their faces; their mittens were unwieldy lumps of ice covering hands that had lost all feeling. To keep on the move took teeth-gritting determination. It was much easier to let the numbness creep up their limbs and into their brain, easier to rest.

"Can't see," one man muttered. Ice on his brows and lashes shuttered his eyes like blinds, and his fingers were too stiff to remove it. In any case, the ice was frozen to the roots of his hair. Many sealers suffered in the same way and stumbled around, blind, until Jesse Collins went from one to the other biting off the lumps of ice with his teeth. He froze his lips doing it.

In the disaster, Jesse had emerged as leader. It was to him the young men turned, rather than to Tuff and Bungay. The officers were somewhere on the pan, but lost in the crowd and the black night.

"Don't give up, fellers, kape on the move," Collins commanded.

"You're the boss, Jesse."

"Awful tired, can't we take a spell?"

"Can't take a spell, b'ys, but we'll bide a while and go fishin'." His voice rose. "Gather round now."

They gathered round, calling to one another in wonder, "Jesse says we're goin' fishin'."

"Get yer jiggers ready, b'ys," he bellowed.

They caught on. Everyone went through the motion of preparing lines and jiggers.

"Ready, Jesse."

Then Jesse commanded them to throw their imaginary lines over the sides of their imaginary boats, then to haul in their lines, hand over hand. With great seriousness they obeyed.

"Catch anything, fellers?"

"Naw, Jesse," they chorused.

"We'll kape tryin', then."

They went through the motions time and again.

"There's not much on the jigger today, b'ys," Jesse roared.

They chorused in agreement, "Naw, nothing' on the jigger."

"Then we'll go with hook and line. Bait up yer hooks."

They obediently baited their imaginary hooks with imaginary squid and threw them into the imaginary sea, pulling in and throwing out until they had the blood coursing through their veins once more.

But even that became wearying after a while, and Jesse roared above the biting wind, "Time to go on parade, b'ys."

They lined up single file and marched round and round the pan, hitting one another on the shoulders, where they felt the cold most of all. Round and round they went, not so fast as to sap their vitality; just a slow shuffling movement to keep the blood circulating.

Jesse Collins seemed to be everywhere, keeping a sharp eye for malingerers; punching, shaking those who were willing to give in: "*Up, b'y, up!*" he would roar with great ferocity, and the men would struggle to their feet to make one more effort to survive.

Numb with cold and exhaustion, young Cecil Mouland still remembered his grandfather's advice about frost-burn. All the while he was obediently "chawing" his tobacco—it would never do to go home to Jessie with a frost-burned face. His new woollen mitts, knitted by his mother, had extended almost to the elbow when he had put them on that morning. But the wet snow and sleet had shrunk them so that now they failed to cover his wrists. Rawhide boots, heavysoled and hobnailed, encased his legs snugly to the knees; but in conditions like these they were obviously not wet proof. He remembered, ruefully, that he had skin cuffs aboard ship, as well as oilskins. "What would I give t' have them oilskins now," he told his cousin Ralph.

"Yah!" Ralph mumbled, and eased himself to the ice. "I'm tired, Cec, gotta take a spell."

Cecil let him rest for a minute only. "That's enough, Ralph." He felt a responsibility for Ralph, since he had persuaded the young man to come to the ice-field with him.

On this same pan, Edward Tippett gathered his two young sons, Norman and Abel, to him. With an arm protectively around each, he did his best to shield them from the cold. Near them Alfred and Bod Maidment, who had earlier that day predicted a record disaster, kept determinedly on the move. Both were married and had children; both were determined to see their families again.

The blizzard of the afternoon was a tea party compared to the one now screaming at them from the north; frost seemed to take their breath, stabbed into their lungs, cut their flesh; there was no facing into that wind.

Numbness gripped even the liveliest, and two strapping young men who laughingly had wrestled strenuously earlier were now reeling from exhaustion. They finally fell to the ice, unable to keep going. But Jesse Collins roused them, forced them to their feet. When they again fell in an exhausted stupor, he kindled a small fire with his greasy rope, cut the top off the molasses can he carried on his belt, and, using snow, made a hot, sweet drink which he shared between the two young men. They revived miraculously, apparently with new life in their bodies. But an hour later their strength gave out again. They fell to the ice and died. The heroic Jesse Collins turned to saving others.

The men, deeply religious, comforted themselves with prayer and hymns. Voices rose quaveringly, singing "Lead, Kindly Light" and "Abide With Me." With great feeling they sang, "Does Jesus Care?"

The savage whine of the wind mocked them.

In Arthur Mouland's shelter, the men fared much better. Thanks to the wing he had forced them to build, they had partial protection in one corner. There they huddled while Mouland, barking above the howling wind, kept them moving their feet, constantly marking time. As they huddled together, numbly marching on the same spot, their body heat did not dissipate and they suffered less discomfort than their unfortunate mates out in the open.

*Newfoundland log:*
*1 a.m. Wind direction North. Wind force 7.*
*Begins with strong gale from north and drifting snow. Ice packed close, and ship jammed.*

The wind backed west of north, and finally held from a point about north by west. All the ice shelters were now completely useless.

The bitter night seemed unending. Each moment was a living hell that dragged interminably on; biting frost and snow rode the gale and the men who could still feel anything suffered unspeakable agony. At some point during the night the snow thinned and finally stopped, but the wind continued to blow with gale force, and ground drift was as blinding as the blizzard had been before.

Great courage was shown on those three ice pans during the dark hours before dawn. Men almost too exhausted to help themselves helped each other. They danced, boxed, and wrestled; they coaxed, wheedled, and rough-housed those who lay on the ice to die. But despite their best efforts, the first grey light revealed many still bodies. Among them were those of William Pear, Bernard and Henry Jordan, Edward Tippett and his two sons, Norman and Abel. Tippett's arms were frozen around his sons' bodies and they still huddled close to him in death. They stood like pieces of sculpture, planted solidly on the ice in a standing embrace, the drifting snow swirling around them.

# CHAPTER TWELVE

*Stephano log:*
*April 1, 5:30 a.m. Heavy NNW gale, blinding snow. Blizzard. Frosty.*

It had been a long night for the crew of the *Stephano* as well. Sleep had been fitful and uneasy for most, and daylight didn't assuage their fears for the safety of the *Newfoundland's* men. Sleep had been impossible for Mark Sheppard, whose approach to Master Watch Gaulton the evening before had given him the status of leader and spokesman for the crew. But his action had produced nothing. The *Stephano* had not budged, and this had unsettled him.

Dawn brought snow squalls, heavy drifting, and fierce winds; the ice-field was one massive boiling witches' cauldron, and the men in number two hold didn't bother to go on deck. They gathered around the bogey, pondering the situation.

"They'm dead out there, ye know that."

It was too horrendous to consider. "Some of 'em, but not *all* of 'em."

"Christ! Man, d'ye think ye could've come through last night, alive?"

"It's Abe Kean's fault. . . ."

"Why don't he go lookin' for 'em?"

"He's a hard man."

A voice cried angrily, "He got no consideration fer the likes of we. What do he care as long as 'e gets he's bloody swiles?"

"I don't understand 'im."

It went on, and Mark listened as anger mounted against Abram Kean. Stories of past grievances were aired and exaggerated, feeding the flame of resentment. But no matter how great their resentment, there was that undercurrent of fear of the Old Man, and no amount of anger could overcome it. When it came right down to brass tacks, not one of them had the courage to confront the captain.

Master Watch Abram Best came down amongst them to collect four men for watch duty. Sheppard asked him, "What do the cap'n think o' the *Newfoundland*'s men?"

Best replied, "He's easy enough about 'em; he thinks they got aboard all right."

"*I'm* sure they didn't," Sheppard said bluntly.

Best stated, "If they didn't, they'm all dead on the ice by now." He picked four men and disappeared topside. It was too rough for work on the ice, and the sealers remained below to chew over the situation. They felt certain that many of the men who had boarded their ship briefly the day before were now frozen to death.

The ice, tight on the land, held the *Stephano* in a vice-like grip.

*Newfoundland log:*

*April 1, 8 a.m. Wind direction North. Wind force 7, barometer 29.50. Strong gale from north and drifting snow. Ice packed close and ship jammed.*

The wind, having backed to the west, was now moving clockwise again.

Bo'sun Tizzard had been up and about the *Newfoundland* by 4 A.M. and was on duty in the barrel as dawn brightened the sky. With the wind still blowing around 38 m.p.h. and the chill factor at −20, it was not the most pleasant spot to be. Drifting snow swirled and eddied with the wind, spinning upwards to the height of fifteen feet. Below Tizzard, the deck of the *Newfoundland* showed dimly through the chiffon veil of snow that whipped and whirled along the flat top. It was, Tizzard thought, too bad a day to be on deck, let alone on the ice.

Wes Kean appeared early and took his stand in the barrel to let Bo'sun Tizzard get breakfast. It was, to Wes, a disappointing day: too rough for hunting, therefore another day lost. Occasionally, as the drifts thinned out, he caught glimpses of the *Stephano* which bore north by east of him. Beyond the *Stephano* he could see the *Florizel*. His glass swept the horizon; to the south there was a three-masted ship which he thought must be the *Diana; to the north-west by west another ship lay—the Bellaventure*, he thought. No ship appeared to be moving, and it was too rough to see if men were working on the ice.

The *Newfoundland* was still jammed, but by the feel of her, she seemed to be riding a little freer. Wes thought that the ice might have loosened slightly during the storm, so when Tizzard returned to the deck Wes ordered steam up. "Bo'sun, you go and scun her through the ice when we get under way. We've got to get to the *Stephano* and pick up our men."

Soon the old ship was quivering under the strain of her pounding engines, pressing forwards and backwards, then ramming full steam ahead to force the ice asunder. But under the terrific strain, the steering chains burst. The ship once more gave up the struggle while Bo'sun Tizzard descended from the barrel to repair the damage.

Captain Joe Kean on the *Florizel* had spent a sleepless night. He had been unable to rest as he listened to the north winds howling through the ship's rigging and he'd sought the comfort of his officers' company. Roberts had eased his mind slightly when the weather had been mild, but the bitter north winds racing across the floes had swept all comforting thoughts aside. If the men *had not* reached their ship (and he greatly feared they had not), human flesh could not possibly withstand the ravages of that wind.

After 1 A.M. he had gone to the chief engineer's cabin for the solace of companionship. John Reader was a friend, and Joe frequently conferred with him. This night, miserably disturbed by the uncertainty of the whole situation, he confessed his anxieties to Reader.

It had been a long night and he was grateful when the sky began to lighten. Again he wished, for the hundredth time, that the *Newfoundland* had wireless.

The lost sealers, sick with exhaustion, could not face into the wind. There could be no question of wandering in blinding drifts to find their ship; to be alive and on their feet was a miracle. To seek their ship was suicide, so they chose to remain where they were until rescuers found them.

On Bungay's pan, sealers shuffled up to Tuff, mute but questioning. Tuff, marking time and hunched against the bitter wind, assured them, "As soon as it clears up, they'll find us."

With the lightening of day they began to wander over the pans in a hopeless search for better shelter. Their numbed, half-frozen bodies were clumsy to manipulate and many fell between ice-floes, wetting feet and legs, but were hauled to safety by companions who still had the wits and strength to help. In many cases the effort was wasted, as shock quickly killed those who had fallen through the ice. Others fell from sheer exhaustion and had to be bullied to their feet; those who were not, died where they lay.

Was it ever going to clear? Snow squalls of blizzard proportion wrapped them in a frosty white world. Drifts had piled several feet high, making walking difficult, but in open spaces the ice was so slick a man would be taken and carried along like an ice-yacht by the wind.

Each minute was a year, interminable, unending. The dead were partially drifted over, and sometimes a sealer, kicking at a hummock of ice to restore life to his feet, discovered to his horror that he was kicking a frozen body. The wind, frost, and drifting snow wore away at the senses, numbed the spirit, and dulled the mind. Hunger pangs added to the misery. The men had not eaten a solid meal in over twenty-four hours; many had no food left; some had a few pieces of hard tack which they shared with their companions. Others nursed along a handful of oatmeal and raisins, quenching their thirst with snow.

It was near mid-morning before Arthur Mouland lost his first man. Charles Warren of New Perlican fell to his knees, clasped his hands in front of him, toppled over, kicked spasmodically for a moment, and then lay still. His companion, Arthur Abbott of Bonavista, dully watched Charlie die, detached and unmoved.

Frightful as the situation was, they were kept alive by the certainty that the whole fleet was scouring the ice-field for them. Hope burned brightly that at any moment a ship would come crunching through the floes. It was a dream, but it kept them going, and while they awaited rescue, Arthur Mouland ordered his men to shift over to the other side of the shelter and to take the corners off and place them on the other side of the wall. Since they were in fairly good condition they managed to do this, but the lee side was now on the hummocky ice, higher and less sheltered from the wind.

On Mouland's pan, young Jacob Dalton watched with disinterest as another young man gave a couple of maniacal shouts, before falling to the ice, dead. No one seemed to notice that he had died; they merely stepped over or walked around the corpse as they shuffled about the pan.

Jesse Collins was still at the work that he had started early the night before, keeping men on their feet and moving. Cecil Mouland was still chewing tobacco, grimly determined to follow his grandfather's advice about keeping his face in motion. His clothes were frozen solid; his muffler, encased in ice, was frozen to his coat. Since he couldn't reach into his pocket—it was frozen shut—he had stuffed the tobacco inside his mitt. When he felt the need for a fresh chew, he worked the plug up the palm of his hand to the wrist, took a bite and let the plug fall back into the mitt again. His chief concern, besides staying alive, was his cousin Ralph, who seemed to be more concerned with resting.

"Cec, I gotta rest," he mumbled, "jest fer five minutes." But Cecil would not let him. Ralph's mother and dad would blame *him* if anything happened to Ralph. Under no circumstances could he allow Ralph to die. "You keep movin', b'y," he croaked.

They shuffled on, following other forms, moving around the dead and dying. Suddenly there appeared before them out of the drifting snow the form of a man crawling on his hands and knees. Slowly, painfully, he came and Cecil recognized him. "It's Ezra Melendy!"

"Uncle" Ezra of Cat Harbour, a quiet man who usually had little to say, was a survivor from the *Greenland* disaster of 1898. Now Cecil noted that he had no mitts. "What are ye doin' on yer hands an' knees, Uncle Ezra?" he asked.

The older man sat back on his heels, holding up two frozen hands. "I lost me mitts an' me hands is wonderful cold," he murmured.

I'll find 'em, sir," Cecil told him and, following Melendy's trail through the snow, found the mitts, as stiff and frozen as the man's hands. "Here they are, Uncle Ezra," Cecil said. "Hold out yer hands an' we'll put 'em on fer ye."

Still kneeling, because his legs were frozen also, Ezra held out his frozen hands, but the stiff icy mitts could not be forced over them. I can't get 'em on," Cecil told him.

"Me hands is awful cold, me son," Ezra murmured. To please him, Cecil took his sculping knife, slit the mitts along the side and fitted them over the frozen hands. Ezra nodded. "That's better."

With his hands covered, Ezra appeared content, "When ye gets back, me son, tell me wife and family that I've gone home." Then he crawled off slowly and painfully into the drifts to die. Soon after, Cecil saw his frozen body on the very edge of the pan. Slush, tossed up by the sea, was covering Uncle Ezra gradually in solid ice.

Reuben Crewe and his son, Albert John, had survived up to now. During the night, whenever the older man showed signs of falling, the boy had rallied long enough to encourage him along, and if the son fell, the older man exerted his failing strength to keep him going. But now, father and son were unable to encourage each other any further. Albert lay on the ice to die, and his father lay beside him, drawing his son's head up under his fisherman's guernsey in a last gesture of protection. Clasped in each other's arms, they died together.

Most of the living owed their lives to Arthur Mouland or Jesse Collins. By contrast, Dawson's pan was a morgue. White mounds littered it from end to end. From the mounds a boot, a hand, a leg extended grotesquely. Survivors coming upon the sight stumbled away, horror in their eyes. Only Dawson, Howlett, Patrick Gosse (Howlett's bunkmate), and Lemuel Squires remained to take advantage of the pitiful shelter of an ice pinnacle. And it was a miracle that Dawson had lived through the night. Having broken trail the day before, he had reached the end of his reserve long since. To make matters worse, he had fallen into the sea three times, wetting feet and legs. Early in the morning he had done a suicidal thing—he had lain on the ice to sleep. He could not be dissuaded; he simply lay on the ice, curled up, and went to sleep. For hours, he lay, immobile; believing that his friend was dead, Lemuel Squires left Dawson's pan.

Now, only John Howlett and Patrick Gosse remained on the pan, and there were too many dead bodies to allow them space to exercise. Howlett, well versed in the art of survival, told Gosse, "We'll shift 'em around to give us a clear path."

Gosse agreed, and they set about moving the bodies so that a clearly defined path lay among the dead. But they had no sooner cleared the way than Gosse pitched forward and lay on the ice without moving. Howlett, who had gone without sleep for more than forty-eight hours, kept falling asleep on his feet, but each time his body hit the ice he woke up. Somehow, he kept getting up, refusing to die.

Many sealers had gravitated to Jacob Bungay's pan where they found Tuff stamping his feet and moving around to keep his circulation going. Now a group of young Carbonear men from

Dawson's watch converged on Tuff; Richard McCarthy and his bunkmate, Albert Kelloway; John Hiscock and his young brother, Joseph Hiscock; all faced Tuff with accusing eyes. "Well, George Tuff, what do you think of it *now*?"

Tuff, in constant motion, replied that it was "turrible bad." Later, with all the survivors of Dawson's pan gravitating to Bungay's to stare in wordless accusation, Tuff could stand it no longer. He broke down and wept. "We're all goin' to be lost and 'tis old Kean's fault!" he declared.

Albert Kelloway died shortly afterwards.

The snow squalls finally stopped but the frost-ridden wind still blew fiercely from the north-north-west, and the drifting continued. Faces were now blistered and purple with frost-burn. Joseph Hiscock, suffering a pleurisy stitch, kept going with the help of his brother, John. Lemuel Squires had again returned to Dawson's pan where he and Howlett surmised that if Dawson wasn't dead, he was not far from it. "I can't get no life to 'im," Howlett said.

Snow drifted and spun skywards, veiling the outside world, and ice and snow crusted the faces of bewhiskered men. Drifts were now waist deep in places, making the struggle for survival more difficult. But still they believed that rescue was at hand, and this belief kept them alive.

"Where's our steamer?"

"Is she comin'?" they croaked to one another.

The morning was passing and more men were dropping. The survivors numbed beyond feeling, decided their chances of survival would be greater if they removed the outer garments from the dead and put them on themselves. A few murmured against this. Among them was James Donovan who was still shuffling around with his brother, Stephen, grimly hanging on to life. Somehow James had lost his cap in the storm the night before, and his hair was matted and spiked with ice and snow. A sealer had fallen and moved again, and as they passed him Stephen had halted, "Take he's cap, Jim."

James shook his head. "No, b'y."

"He don't need it, Jim, you do," Stephen coaxed.

James was stubborn. "It's not right to take from the dead," he said, and no amount of persuasion could make him change his mind.

Despite such protests, the instinct for survival among the men was stronger than their queasiness about wearing the clothing of dead men. Mufflers, caps, and jackets were pried or cut from the dead, and wrapped about the living.

Many now drifted towards Arthur Mouland's pan, and Arthur set them to work building their own shelters. Not that he expected to be on the ice another night, but he was a practical man who felt that if the weather did not abate, another night out might be possible. Besides, it kept the men active. So far, his own watch had suffered the fewest casualties, with just two men dead.

Cecil Mouland, still on Bungay's pan, now had his hands full with his cousin, Ralph. Many of their companions had given in to weariness, muttering that they were going to take five minutes' rest. "Jest five minutes," they vowed, and meant it. But, sitting hunched to keep warm, most of them had toppled over dead within minutes.

Ralph gave up finally and lay on the ice ready to call it quits. But Cecil still was not prepared to let him go. He shuffled over to him, knelt and roused him, "You goin' to die, Ralph?"

Ralph croaked wearily, "Yes, Cecil, I can't stick it no longer." By now Cecil didn't have the physical strength to force Ralph to his feet, but again the accusing eyes of his aunt and uncle seemed to follow him. "I wouldn't die if I was you. I wouldn't give it to 'em to say at home, b'y, that you died out on this ol' ice," he coaxed, then he clumsily manipulated his sack and hauled out one of his cakes of hard bread. "Eat some hard tack," he urged, "that'll give you strength."

Ralph had no interest in hard tack, since he hadn't the strength to bite into it. He just wanted to be left alone to die. He closed his eyes.

"I'll chew it fer you," Cecil coaxed.

He bit into the hard tack, chewed until it was sufficiently thawed, and transferred the softened morsel to his cousin's mouth. In this way he gave Ralph enough strength to stagger to his feet and carry on. Once, in their shuffling around the pan, Cecil found himself face to face with Tuff, the leader who had landed them in the midst of this disaster. "Well, Skipper George, what do you think of all this?" he croaked. It wasn't polite conversation, and indeed it was as close to an accusation as Cecil's nature allowed.

Tuff told Cecil, "B'y, I don't think ther'll be a man left to tell the tale."

Jessie's face floated before Cecil's eyes. "Well, I'm not goin' to die, George," he said, and turning, walked away, dragging a resigned Ralph with him.

*Stephano log:*

*Wed. Apr. 1. Ship unable to pick up pans, very frosty weather. 10 a.m. Ship under way making very slow progress. Noon, heavy gale continued, weather clearing, ship picking up pans with much difficulty.*

It had been a rough morning, so bad that even the Old Man didn't consider putting his men out to haul seals aboard—not even the ones belonging to the *Florizel*, a hundred yards off his port bow. It was a worrisome day to him, because it was likely that half their uncollected pans were lost in the storm—foundered maybe, or miles away in wheeling ice. He had given no thought to the *Newfoundland* crew. They hadn't come to him last evening, so he assumed that they had found their way back to their ship. That being so, he wasted no time thinking of them.

By 10 A.M. *Stephano* was butting through heavy ice making little headway towards that *Florizel* flag and pan of seals, and it was obvious it was going to be an unproductive day. Getting up to noon it began to brighten as the snow squalls ceased, but it was still too rough to work, and the Old Man envisioned his pans wheeling around the ice-field, ready to be pirated by the first ship that came along. He went to the wireless shack and said to Shecklin the operator, "Tell the *Florizel* to pick up any of our pans they come across, and tell 'em to keep a tally of 'em."

"Righto, Cap'n!" Shecklin said, and promptly set about it.

The Old Man, returning to the bridge, ordered the deck hands over the side, "Bring the *Florizel*'s pan aboard."

The men had barely disappeared into the drifts before another flag was reported off the starboard bow, and men were dispatched to tow the pelts aboard. No one then gave this flag off the starboard bow a second thought. But later it proved important in establishing the *Stephano's* approximate position at this time, which was farther southward than the Old Man thought. Yetman's idea of their position was far more accurate than Abram Kean's.

The ship manoeuvred back and forth, and presently, with much difficulty, began to force her way through the ice. Below deck her crew still fretted about the *Newfoundland*'s men.

*Newfoundland log:*
*Noon: Wind direction NNW. Wind force 7. Barometer 29.60. Strong gale and sky clearing.*

It had been a quiet morning aboard the *Newfoundland*. The men were depressed with the belief that their mates were dead or dying; most likely all dead. The empty hold seemed like a morgue, the meagre belongings, stowed on the bunks, now seemed personal effects of the departed.

With haggard eyes, Jordan stared at the empty tin mug in his fist. He hadn't slept, hadn't rested, wasn't even remotely tired. Every sense, every nerve, was alert . . . and aware of disaster. He *knew*!

Bo'sun Tizzard had repaired the wheel chains, the ice had loosened slightly, and Wes had ordered steam up. "We'll try to get up to the *Stephano* to pick up our men," he told Tizzard. The bo'sun went to the holds and ordered, "All hands on deck! We're goin' to pick up our crew aboard the *Stephano* as soon as we get up steam."

It was 2 P.M. when they crawled out of the holds to face the gale winds and drifting snow spinning around their ship in furious gusts. Tizzard allocated so many to shovelling snow, and so many to passing coal from the bunkers to the engine room. The men worked with a will, glad of the physical activity that demanded their undivided attention. At last they were doing something useful.

*Florizel* log:

*Apr. 1. 11 a.m. Full speed at 10:45 a.m. Blowing a gale with snowstorm, cleared up at 10:30 a.m. still blowing heavy. Picking up scattered seals.*

Captain Joe Kean was still uneasy. The continuing storm not only left the fate of the *Newfoundland*'s men unknown, but seemed to have scattered his pans of precious pelts. It was difficult moving around in the ice and the *Florizel*'s propellor kept hitting the pans heavily, sending shudders through the steel ship. It was evident that they weren't going to make much progress today.

The *Bellaventure* (of Harvey's fleet, like the *Newfoundland*) was still southward of the string of seals, about where she had been the day before when Wes's men were marching over the ice. Captain Robert Randell, having been informed by the *Bonaventure* where the seals lay, was anxious to reach them and get in on the spoils, but the ice to the northward had closed up tight. He was still able to move freely about in his own part of the ice-field, however. The *Stephano*, bearing about east-north-east three miles, didn't appear to be moving about much. Occasionally, as his men sighted scattered seals a gunshot or so away, he steamed as closely as possible to them and let his men go after them.

The survivors, still awaiting rescue, were southward of the *Bellaventure*.

It was between snow squalls and past noon when Tuff, scanning the horizon for signs of rescue ships during the brief lull, thought he saw the two barrels of the *Newfoundland* to the leeward. The drift was still high and the swirling snow was deceptive, but he was sure it was the *Newfoundland*; *it had to be*. He felt that their troubles were nearly over and called to those men who were still on their feet, "Good news, men, I b'lieve I seen our steamer right to le'ward."

They heard him apathetically, almost past the stage of caring about living or dying. Eyes swollen and blinded by the wind were no longer able to search. The men were more dead than alive. Tuff continued, "I'll take one or two men with me and go half a mile further along. If th' driftin' lets up again I'll have a better chance to see her." He cautioned, "But I don't want anyone else to leave the pan or to scatter. Everyone is to stay here until help comes."

Sidney Jones stepped forward. "I'll go with you, sir."

"Me too, Skipper." Henry Dowden also stepped forward.

Joshua Holloway was of two minds, to go with Tuff or to stay where he was. Then he reasoned that he was better off to remain where he was. His brother Philip was also on the pan.

Tuff, Jones, and Dowden ventured from their scant shelter, confident that they were in the immediate vicinity of their ship since they must have passed her closely the night before. But a hundred yards from their shelter they were caught by the gale force winds and blown helplessly about the ice until they reached the shelter of an ice rafter about two hundred yards from the rest of the crowd. For safety's sake, they stayed there, because it was impossible to race into the wind to get back to their own pan.

The drifting snow still hid the *Newfoundland*.

They stayed there in the scant shelter afforded by the rafter for an hour until the wind began to slacken and the drifting to cease. Bungay, from their old pan, saw them, "I'm goin' to j'in Skipper George," he told the men around him.

"So will I," said Jesse Collins. "Anyone else comin'?"

They were joined by Philip Holloway and Stanley Andrews, and the four men tracked the three to their sheltering rafter.

Tuff met them with a reprimand. "You'd have been better off staying where you were."

It was true. The seven of them huddled beneath the ice rafter, finding it too bitterly cold to face into the wind. Soon Henry Dowden and Philip Holloway reached the limit of their endurance and lay on the ice to die. Presently, the wind slacked a little more and the others decided to try and find more adequate shelter. "It seems to me there's a rafter of ice yonder that'd protect us a bit more," Tuff said.

Dowden and Holloway could not rise, and Tuff and his little band left. It *was* better shelter and the wind was decreasing somewhat, giving them clear visibility for about two miles when they climbed an ice pinnacle to look for a ship. Keeping a constant check to the leeward where he thought he had seen the *Newfoundland*, Tuff at last came to the bitter conclusion that there was no ship there. He clumsily backed down off the ice pinnacle, reluctant to look into their burning eyes. "B'ys, I gotta tell ye, there's no ship handy to us at all."

To Tuff it seemed incredible that every ship in the icefield was not converging on them. He was convinced that they must be combing the ocean for them, but that drifting snow was obscuring them from the rescue ships. With this conviction he did not discourage easily, but kept a sharp lookout, his eyes sweeping the limited horizon around them. About mid-afternoon the skies cleared and the drifting began to die down. The sun broke through the overcast, so piercingly bright and beautiful it hurt their eyes. With renewed hope, Tuff climbed an ice pinnacle, his eyes searching . . . searching.

His voice tore through the cold air. *"We're saved! There's a steamer coming fer us!"*

Sure enough, a couple of miles to the windward (the north-west), looming through the drifting snow was a big, beautiful steel ship, the most beautiful sight he'd ever seen in his life. "It's the *Ad* . . . the good ol' *Adventure*," he croaked.

It was actually the *Bellaventure*, steaming at random, picking up scattered families of hoods—but she was steaming directly for them.

Now there was hope and cheer. It was only a matter of time before they would all be on board ship with a hot meal tucked beneath their belts and a snug berth beneath their tired bodies. Visions of hot food made them realize just how starved they were.

"She'm a good piece away," murmured one.

Tuff agreed, "I 'low she's about two mile." He could feel new life coursing through his body. "Cheer up, men, we'm ahl rate," he exhorted. "We'll be aboard a steamer in jig time; that captain'll see us and come to us."

With rescue so near he could not bear the thought of standing still and waiting it out. He felt the need to hurry towards her, to get aboard quickly and hurry her on to pick up the men before more died. He made a swift decision and turned to Jones, "Sidney, you bide here and take charge of the two sick men. Jesse Collins is about the smartest man here, I'll take 'im an' go aboard. When we get aboard we'll come fer ye as quick as we can."

Tuff and Collins started off in the direction of the ship. Bungay followed after a moment, leaving Jones and Andrews to make it back to the first shelter under the ice rafter where Henry Dowden and Philip Holloway lay on the ice. Dowden was Jones's friend and he did his best to rouse the unconscious young man. "Wake up, Henry b'y, we'm save," he coaxed.

Arthur Mouland's watch was the most westerly, and he was, consequently, closest to the *Bellaventure* as she steamed in their direction. When he saw her Arthur didn't waste time. He gave his men strict orders to keep in the ice shelter as much as they could. Then, taking his cousin Elias Mouland and Samuel Russell (both of Bonavista), he headed for the *Bellaventure*. Sam, a bit lame because of an accident the year before, lagged and fell behind. Arthur told him, "Come on at yer own pace, we'll hurry on the the *Bell* . . . Take care."

They were soon well ahead of Samuel and moving at a swift pace towards the ship.

The main group, which consisted now of the survivors of Dawson's, Bungay's, and Jones's watches, were scattered between the two pans. On Dawson's pan, John Howlett and Lemuel Squires huddled beneath the shelter of the pinnacle; around them, bodies lay still beneath a coverlet of snow. By now wind and wave had opened the ice, making travel treacherous for the weakened, exhausted men. Snow added to the treachery, blanketing open water between pans, making it look like solid ice.

James Ryan and Michael Tobin were two Fermeuse men who had made it easily through the night, confident that they would survive. But today had been a different story. James was weakening; twice he had fallen through the ice and each time Michael had hauled him to safety. It was Michael who coaxed him along, Michael who tried to rub the circulation back into James's frozen legs. Then Michael coaxed him to his feet and sang their favorite songs as they staggered around the ice-floes.

Joseph Hiscock was in a bad way. The pleurisy stitch was like a knife in his side; his bunkmate had died, and Joe was taking it badly. He had pleaded with his brother John, "I don't want to stay on the same pan with him," but was powerless to move on his own. John and his buddy Richard McCarthy had obliged the youth, taking him to the leeward, passing pans with dead and dying men, until they found a pan with a handful of men under an ice pinnacle that sheltered them slightly from the wind. Among this group was an old friend, Henry Kelloway, and here they had remained until the snow stopped and the drifting moderated.

Miraculously the sky cleared, and above the drift they saw the sun shining in all its glory. John Hiscock shouted, "We're goin' t'have it fine." He went around giving cheer and encouragement. "Cheer up! It's fine now." But for the most part the others seemed to be beyond caring, and John, determined to find the nearest steamer, climbed the ice pinnacle to gaze over the drifting snow. To the leeward, where it was easier to see, there was nothing, but to the windward, where the frosty wind cut his face and eyes, the spars of a ship stuck straight up through the drift. "It's a steamer!" he shouted.

The men halted their slow shuffle, hope gleaming in their wind-cut eyes. "Come on, fellers, let's go fer her," Hiscock urged.

"Where is she?" one croaked.

"To the windward, a couple mile."

They stood there, stupefied by cold and exhaustion. It might as well have been a couple of hundred miles. The ice had loosened, showing dark swatches of water, swatches that would have presented no problem to fresh, able sealer, but that looked as wide as an ocean to these dying men. They barely had strength enough to stand, let alone travel over loose ice. On top of that, the *Bellaventure* was to the windward—a couple of miles, they said. Who had the strength to walk in the teeth of a gale?

"Well?" Hiscock urged. He wanted badly to get aboard, to get help for Joe, but he was well aware of the folly of venturing alone across the ice in his weakened condition.

McCarthy said readily, "I'll go."

It was enough, he had needed only one other. Hiscock turned to his young brother. "Will you come too, Joe?"

Joe nodded feebly. "I'll try."

With shoulders hunched and heads down, they staggered along in the teeth of the wind, Joe favouring his paining side. They didn't get far before he doubled over, gasping, "I can't go no farther."

Hiscock and McCarthy wasted no time in argument. They simply took Joe by the arms and carried him along. Suddenly, Hiscock gave a cry of fright as his feet went through slush and snow, and the icy sea flooded his boots. Instinctively, he flung himself forward, clawing the ice with his gaff. McCarthy leapt to his aid and hauled him onto solid ice.

The two of them wasted no time, but took Joe's arms and weaved across the floes till they came to one which contained a number of men standing forlornly among a number of frozen bodies. It was here that Joe gave up, gasping with pain. "I can't go a step farther."

"Come on, Joe, it's not far. The steamer's not far away," Hiscock lied.

Joe's face was twisted with pain, "The stitch is . . . too bad fer me to take . . . another step," he muttered and tumbled like a sack to the ice, where he laboured for breath.

"I'll go on fer help," McCarthy said

Hiscock, bending anxiously over his brother, looked up to warn McCarthy, "Don't go be yerself, the ice is too loose. If ye falls in ther'll be nobody to get you out."

McCarthy nodded. "Yah!" He went to the men standing among the dead. "Anyone ready to try an' get aboard that ship with me?"

No one was. They were too far gone to expend their last vestige of strength on the rough trek over the ice. McCarthy wasted no more time with them. Instead, "See the steamer?"

They indicated that they had.

"I'm goin' to board her—ye comin' with me?"

Lemuel Squires said promptly, "I'll come," but Howlett hesitated, then shook his head. "Not me, b'ys, I'll wait till they pick us up."

"Let's go, then." McCarthy and Squires hunched their shoulders against the bitter wind, headed into the teeth of the gale and were almost immediately lost to sight in the drifting snow. . . .

By now all the survivors on the ice knew about the *Bellaventure*, and men who had been ready to give up felt the thrust of new life. Cecil and Ralph Mouland were among them. Cecil, in his exuberance, found the strength to climb an ice pinnacle. There before his eyes, over the undulating ice and drifting snow, was the *Bell* steaming slowly towards them. Below him, Ralph, standing on frozen legs, watched him anxiously.

"Is she comin'?" he asked.

"She'm comin', Ralph, she'm comin'," Cecil shouted happily.

The *Bell*, crawling along, turned away to starboard, and the new life drained away from Cecil. But presently the *Bell* turned again, obviously following leads in the ice as she turned to starboard and port, but still coming nearer. Cecil swung from the heights of rapture to the depths of despair as the *Bell* manoeuvred through the ice, but he had no doubts whatever that they had been found.

With McCarthy gone, John Hiscock turned his full attention to Joe. He knelt beside his brother, removed his mitts, and with clumsy hands took the last handful of oatmeal from his bag. Mixing it with Radways, he fed it to Joe with his fingers. Joe ate thankfully, and the hot liniment filled his belly with the illusion of warmth. He seemed to revive a little.

When the last crumb of oatmeal was gone, Hiscock rose to his feet to take his bearings. Nearby was Dawson's pan, where they had spent the night. Dawson had been pretty near gone when he'd last seen him, where was he now? They were both Carbonear men and good friends.

"You rest, Joe, I'll be back in a minute," Hiscock said, then made his way to the pan. Among the white mounds of dead Howlett was the only man there on his feet. "How's Skipper Tom?" he asked Howlett, who pointed to the still body of Dawson. "He's sleepin'."

*Sleeping?* Hiscock was incredulous. He bent stiffly to his knees and shook the still form. "Skipper! Skipper!"

He kept calling, and presently Dawson stirred slightly. "Skipper, there's a steamer alongside," Hiscock croaked urgently.

Dawson croaked back, "A steamer?" He struggled to rise.

"McCarthy is gone to her fer help," Hiscock told him, helping him to his knees.

Satisfied that Dawson's senses were returning and that he was now all right, Hiscock left the pan to return to Joseph who was lying on the ice, waiting anxiously. "John, I can't die here, take me clear o' the dead men," he pleaded.

"You won't die, Joe,'" Hiscock promised. "I'll get Henry Kelloway to help us get away from here." He went back quickly to the remnants of Bungay's watch where he found Kelloway standing dejectedly beneath the pinnacle. "Can you walk, Henry?"

Henry nodded and John urged, "Help me with Joe so we can find a pan where they might have a fire going?"

Henry agreed. When the two of them reached Joseph, they picked him up and tried to drag him over the ice, but once again, under the burden of his brother, John fell into the sea. This time Kelloway hauled him out, but Joe lay on the ice and could not be roused. Wet, numb, and exhausted, Hiscock shook and pleaded with Joe to keep going. But Joe was beyond hearing.

"It's no use, John," Kelloway told him gently. "He can't hear ye."

"No," Hiscock agreed, and sat beside his brother.

"Will we go on?" Kelloway asked. "We could try to carry 'im."

"We might lose 'im in the sea, Henry. So we'll stay."

The wind screamed over the ice, and Henry Kelloway returned to his shelter while Hiscock, with all the spark and ginger gone out of him, sat beside his brother to watch him die. He was suddenly past caring about living or dying—or anything, for that matter. No wind penetrated the ice that sheathed his body. Now he felt curiously warm and comfortable, and so tired he simply had to rest.

He stretched out on the ice and lay beside Joseph.

# CHAPTER THIRTEEN

George Tuff, Jacob Bungay, and Jesse Collins were headed for the *Bellaventure*. It was still blowing fiercely, with a wind chill factor of $-20$, and a low drift that limited visibility. But hope gave wings to their feet. Tuff was again supremely confident that their plight was known to the world at large and that rescue was at hand. He dispensed encouragement left and right as he passed among the sealers: "We'm saved men; 'tis all over; we'm saved."

They heard, and life returned to the dying.

"It won't be long now, men; the *Bell* is comin'—she'll be here in no time." To the ablest he said, "Put yer flags up; stick 'em on a pinnacle."

Once, in his eagerness, jumping from pan to pan. Tuff fell into the sea, but he scrambled back to the ice without aid, anxious to cover the distance to the ship. "I'm ahl rate," he told Bungay and Collins, moving smartly on.

The remnants of the crew were pitiful indeed. On one pan *all* were dead, lying grotesque and silent, a floating cemetery through which they sped uncaring, their emotions numbed by suffering. Beyong that ghastly ice pan the living mingled with the dead, standing like lost souls in an alien world, only the faintest thread of hope still tying them to reality. Confident and encouraging, Tuff came among them: "The *Bell*'s comin' fer us, men; stick yer flags to the pinnacles so they'll find us sooner."

They stared at him, eyes puffed, swollen, and glazed faces blistered by frost and wind, and made no motion to obey. Tuff told Bungay and Collins: "Look fer a flag; we'll put it up fer 'em."

They found a flag and a pair of overalls, half buried in a drift. The overalls (removed from one of the dead) were as stiff as the body from which they had come. "We'll put 'em both up," Tuff said grimly, and soon the flag and frozen overalls were flying in the wind.

They continued north-west towards Master Watch Mouland's shelter, and several of Mouland's men came to meet them, "Mr. Tuff . . .?"

"Where's Arthur?"

"We come to tell ye, sir, he started off fer the *Bell* long ago."

"How long?"

"They must be nearly aboard now, sir."

"Who went with 'im?"

"Elias Mouland and Sam Russell, sir."

"We'd better take a look an' see how they're doin'," Tuff said to Bungay and Collins. They climbed the nearest ice pinnacles to see if they could sight the men.

Richard McCarthy and Lemuel Squires arrived at Mouland's shelter about then. Learning that others were already approaching the *Bell*, they waited.

From their pinnacle Tuff, Bungay, and Collins could see Mouland and one of his men, well over a mile away, approaching the ship, which now seemed to have stopped. The third man was well to the rear.

Huddling beneath them in the sparse shelter of the pinnacle the ghastly, ice-caked remnants of those who had wandered to Mouland's pan croaked hopefully, "Is she comin' yet?"

The drift had died down considerably, but snow still spun about, settling into the creases of their frozen clothing, and they looked less than human. "When will she be here, Skipper?"

How could Tuff tell them she had stopped, that she wasn't steaming full-speed in their direction? He eased himself down. "I'm goin' to try an' get aboard," he told them.

"I'll come," Bungay said.

"Me too." Collins moved beside him.

McCarthy and Squires, meantime, had been collecting discarded gaffs and flagpoles, and were trying to light a fire.

"Let's go," McCarthy suggested.

Squires, intent on building the fire, decided to remain.

"I'll follow Tuff, then." McCarthy rose and hurried after the three men.

"Where are *you* goin'?" Tuff growled, as he came abreast.

"To the *Bell*."

"You may give out," Tuff warned.

"I can go as well as the next man," McCarthy insisted.

But they got only a short distance. The ice was loose, free-floating, making it very difficult for men in their weakened condition.

"We're goin' to have to go back," Tuff decided.

The *Bellaventure* had steamed about the ice-field in the vicinity of the lost party spotting scattered seals and dropping men to pick them up. Once they had glimpsed the *Stephano* to the north-north-east, but after that, nothing. The weather slowly cleared, and she steamed slowly southward, stopping as some scattered seals were sighted, waiting as the men killed them and brought the pelts aboard. It was between three and four o'clock when Abram Parsons, the second hand, sighted the *Newfoundland* through drifts, several miles to the eastward. The *Bellaventure* had remained stationary for some considerable time while they loaded seal pelts. Then, since there were more live seals nearby, they decided to leave three men on the spot to finish off the patch while she steamed farther afield.

Arthur Mouland and Elias Mouland were now so near the *Bellaventure* that they could see a man on the bulwarks, but they had run into loose ice while still a quarter of a mile from the ship, and had to halt. To get nearer they would have had to swim.

"We're handy enough to signal at any rate," Arthur said to Elias.

He still carried his gaff, and Elias had a flag of the *Newfoundland* wrapped around his neck. Arthur took the flag, tied it to the gaff, and began to wave it vigorously, from the top of a high ice pinnacle that rose well above the drifting snow. Elias, on another pinnacle, waved his arms. Both shouted, but the wind carried their voices away.

The *Bellaventure*, broadside to them, maddeningly close, was putting men on the ice over the far side. No one looked in the direction of the two men trying frantically to attract their attention beyond the stretch of open water. Soon the big ship wheeled around, turned her stern to them, and steamed away. She left behind three sealers working diligently in the seals. They were less than a quarter mile away across open water but they did not once look in the direction of the frantic, lost men.

Arthur and Elias could only stare hopelessly after the *Bellaventure* as she steamed northward, vanishing like a phantom ship into the drifting snow. Arthur was a sight, with his moleskin pants split at the seams and his red flannel underwear coming through, mute testimony to the hardship of the past two days.

He said grimly to Elias, "Looks like we're not going to get aboard any ship till we get to our own."

The weather was clearing rapidly, the ground drift was settling, and a wintry sun was casting deep shadows over the ice-floes. Scanning the horizon, Arthur noted a pillar of heavy smoke some six or seven miles to the south-south-east. "That's the smoke of our own ship," he said.

"Yah!" Elias agreed.

In spite of the fact that they were less than a quarter of a mile from a party of sealers working on the ice, they decided there was only one thing to do—retrace their steps, and head for the *Newfoundland*.

"Still jammed, be the looks of her," Arthur said, "but if she breaks free she'll be comin' fer us."

He handed the flag back to Elias, who wrapped it around his neck again. "We might be able to walk aboard 'fore dark," he suggested. On such a bright day as it now was there would be more than two hours of daylight, yet.

They started to walk to the *Newfoundland*.

As the *Bellaventure* turned and steamed away, young Cecil Mouland, spying her from an ice pinnacle, couldn't believe his eyes. His hopes had gone up and down as she steamed about in the vicinity, and he kept telling himself that she was working her way through the ice, having actually spotted them. When she turned around and disappeared he felt utterly abandoned, cast away; he just couldn't bear it.

"Will she be here soon?" It was Ralph's voice breaking in on his gloom.

He dropped wearily down to the ice pan.

"She's gone away," he said gruffly. He put his arm through Ralph's. "Come on, b'y, get movin'."

From Mouland's pan, too, they had been watching Arthur and Elias. Squires had started a small fire there, around which the frozen sealers clustered. Tuff had endeavoured to start another fire, but couldn't find a dry match. Mockingly, the clatter of the *Bell*'s deck winches came to them plainly.

"Is the steamer comin' yet?" they asked anxiously.

"Yes, she's comin'," Tuff lied. It had the effect of keeping the men cheerful.

He was watching from the pinnacle when the ship turned north.

"Is she comin'?" they asked.

He did not answer as he dropped back to the ice, trying to summon up the courage to tell them the stark truth. He waited to be sure Arthur Mouland was returning before he broke the news to them: "Men, Arthur is coming back. The steamer is gone away."

He realized, then, for the first time, that *nobody was looking for them*. Nobody knew that they were lost on the ice. Every soul of them might die, before anyone even knew they were missing!

Several of them died within minutes of learning that the ship was not coming. Their weariness was suddenly too much for them. They lay on the ice "to rest fer a minute," and never moved again.

The dying men were too much for Tuff. He climbed the pinnacle again. His eyes burned with hope as he saw that the *Stephano* was heading their way. She was farther away than the *Bell* had been, but near enough so that Tuff could see the ice churning up from her prow.

"It's ahl rate, men, it's ahl rate!" he shouted. "Cap'n Kean sees us an' he's comin'. The *Stephano* is headin' this way."

Hope was bright again, and it seemed to relight the flame of life in the dying.

"Is she handy?" they asked. "She's not far, is she?"

"She's comin' men," Tuff comforted. The ship was turning back and forth, still heading south. Though the ice was loose here, it must be tight where the *Stephano* was.

"She's lookin' fer a good lead to come fer us, b'ys," he reported. He continued his lookout, eyes straining eagerly. And soon she wheeled. And then he could see her stern. She, too, was steaming away.

Again he dropped back to the ice and faced the men. Looking into the questioning, hopeful faces, he said quietly, "Cap'n Kean is not comin' either, men. He's gone away, too."

Emptiness returned to eyes where hope had flickered a moment before. Minds that had groped back to reality, retreated again into fantasy. They shuffled on, around the floes, husks of men that would soon drop and rise no more.

Tuff could not look at them. Instead, he returned to his ice pinnacle, his eyes searching the horizon, until they came to rest on the *Newfoundland*. She was a good four miles away, he decided. She did not appear to be moving. It was now about an hour to sunset, a good two hours until dark. The ice glinted red and gold in the low wintry sun.

The *Newfoundland* was still trapped, he decided. She would have to remain where she was, and so they could walk to her. If they were going to reach any ship, this was the logical one.

He told them. "The *Newfoundland* is about four miles from us. She seems to be still jammed. I want the smartest men on this pan to come with me. We'll try to reach her."

The word was passed around, but to most of them the *Newfoundland* might as well have been the moon. Four miles over broken ice and snowdrifts? Most of them could barely stand.

But Bungay came forward, followed by Squires. "We'll go, Skipper."

Jacob Dalton, a member of Mouland's watch, also stepped forward. Tuff turned to Jesse Collins, "Jesse . . .?"

But Collins elected to remain where he was. "I'll wait here with the men, George." Perhaps he guessed that they would still have need of those deep resources of strength that he could draw upon to fight despair.

Tuff nodded. "If the *Newfoundland* is jammed, we'll get on board of her some time tonight. Perhaps Cap'n Wes will see us comin' over the ice. If so we'll all be saved. The rest of ye'll stay here and do yer best to stay alive. If we get on board ye'll have help right away."

With that they moved off smartly. They were followed by a fourth man who hurried to catch up. It was Eli Kean, a relative of the Old Man's.

Richard McCarthy had decided to walk to the *Newfoundland*, too. But he couldn't go alone, so he headed for the pan where he had left his good friends, the Hiscock brothers. To his dismay, both were lying on the ice, apparently dead. Joe did not respond to his shaking, but John eventually did, and McCarthy dragged him to his feet.

"What about the *Bell*?" Hiscock asked groggily.

"She's gone out o' sight, but the *Newfoundland* is to the loo'ard, an' Tuff's gone to her."

"Then we'll go too," Hiscock decided. He actually seemed refreshed by his short sleep. He reached to waken his brother.

"Joe's dead," McCarthy told him.

John nodded, accepting it dumbly. Before leaving, they decided to put Joe's body with the other dead sealers—the ones he had earlier tried to get away from. But they discovered that they lacked the strength to carry the body over the ice. They dragged it, together, to the centre of the pan so there would be no danger of its rolling into the sea. Then they headed for their ship.

Tuff, Bungay, Squires, Dalton, and Eli Kean passed once more among the dead and dying sealers. They moved purposefully, for time was now short. As Tuff travelled eastward, Sidney Jones and Stanley Andrews, and who had remained to comfort the dying Henry Dowden and Philip Holloway, took off to join him and his small crew. Henry and Philip were dead. Behind Tuff's party McCarthy and Hiscock hurried eastward. To the north, heading in a straight line for their ship, were Arthur Mouland, Elias Mouland, and Sam Russell. Twelve of the sealers were thus heading for the *Newfoundland* in three separate groups.

The frosty wind knifed at them from behind, and the ice was rough. They were back, now, in the heavy Arctic ice which, driven by storm currents, had wheeled and changed its position, just as their ship had done. Tuff, in a desperate hurry, misjudged his footing several times and slipped into the water. But by now a wetting seemed incidental to him, and inconvenience only, not the edge of disaster, as he would have regarded it three days ago.

They had covered the first mile in good time when suddenly Eli Kean's strength gave out, and he sank to the ice.

"I can't make it, George, can't go on."

"Are ye sure?" Tuff urged.

"Yah. Ye go on. . . ." He waved them forward.

Tuff hesitated. Stanley Andrews had volunteered to stay behind with Pear, early the previous evening—it seemed ages ago. Now he turned to Andrews again:

"Stay with him, Stan. We'll send back help as soon as we get to the ship. We can't waste time now. Everyone's lives depend on it. We got to leave you, Eli."

Eli nodded, and they passed on, leaving Andrews with him. As they vanished among the rafters, Eli sat on a hummock and said to his companion: "You can't do any good fer me, Stan, so you go on, me son, and tell Skipper George to send out a kettle of tea when he gets on board."

Stanley did not have to be urged. Leaving Kean partly sheltered among the pressure ridges, he hurried after Tuff. The second mile had passed, and the sun had set, when he caught up with them. He gave Tuff Eli's message, and the second hand nodded. Two miles to go . . . they could make it by dark.

McCarthy and Hiscock came upon Eli Kean sitting on the ice. They stopped long enough to find out who he was, then hurried after Tuff.

The sky in the west was still bright and stained with colour when the two Moulands and Sam Russell converged on Tuff's party. They all judged the ship to be about two miles away. Another hour or two . . . Meanwhile, their chances of being seen from the barrel were just about gone.

"Never mind," Tuff consoled the men. "If the ship keeps her lights up we'll have no trouble reachin' her."

But suddenly the *Newfoundland*, belching heavy black smoke, began to steam away from them. The impossible had happened! After all this time jammed in the ice, she had finally broken free, just as they needed her so desperately to stay where she was! She was moving off to the northward towards the *Stephano*. No one would see the little cluster of figures, two miles away in the rough ice on her port beam. Her course would not take her near the dead and dying sealers on the pans. It was the end. George Tuff sat down on the ice and put his head on his knees and wept.

McCarthy and Hiscock had caught up with the little band of men at last, and the eleven of them stared unbelievingly at their ship as she vanished into the dusk.

Tuff was thinking, privately, that it was just as well for them to stay and die where they were as to walk any farther. First the *Bellaventure*, than the *Stephano*, now their own ship, had abandoned them in turn; they had gotten no rest for two days; their bodies and brains had been strained to the point of collapse; fate had handed them one cruel blow after another. They would not live—could not, surely, live—another night on the ice with that cruel wind from the north-west.

"We may as well fix away a place fer us to die," Tuff said.

They sought shelter beneath an ice rafter with two pinnacles sticking out of it. The wind howled between the pinnacles, chilling the blood in their veins.

But Arthur Mouland was still not anxious to die sooner than necessary. He recalled that a little way back they had passed an ice rafter offering more shelter. It had a niche where the wind could not reach them.

"Let's go to it," he suggested.

They did, winding among the hummocks and upended pans until they came to the rafter he had chosen. Tuff immediately climbed it to see if, miraculously, a ship had appeared somewhere near by. There was none, of course; but looking two miles back to the party on the pans, he could see that the *Bellaventure* was returning. At that distance it looked as if she were right among the men.

"The *Bell*'s back, an' she's pickin' up the b'ys!" he shouted.

The others came swarming up the rafter. The last stains of red and gold silhouetted the ship and the distant party of lost sealers.

"She's pickin' up the b'ys," Tuff said. "We'll be the only ones left on the ice. She's pickin' 'em up, and *here we are*, two miles away."

One by one they wordlessly slid down the rafter into the shelter below. They now faced another night on the ice, and the thought was almost too much for them to endure. All day they had been subjected to winds with a −20 chill factor. Now, with darkness, the cold seemed to increase.

The *Bellaventure* had returned to pick up her three men and the pelts they had panned late that afternoon. Her winches squalled as she hoisted the pelts, and Second Hand Abram Parsons, from his position on the bridge, idly scanned the horizon to leeward. The drift had now stopped, and the fading daylight he fancied he saw a few men working the seals a mile or so distant. Was it the *Newfoundland*'s crew? He did not have the spy-glasses with him, so instead of pursuing the matter, he turned back to the work at hand. Soon the pelts were on board and the *Bellaventure* steamed off northward again.

She had not discovered the lost men, as Tuff had thought. Once more she had missed them by a hairsbreadth.

The *Newfoundland*'s engines had pounded ceaselessly most of the afternoon as the ship pressed backwards and forwards trying to free herself. Just before sunset, she succeeded. She wheeled north-north-west towards the *Stephano*, able to manoeuvre in the ice at last. It was a jubilant Wes Kean who went to his supper, confident that he would soon reclaim his men from the *Stephano* and have them back on his own ship that night.

At 8 P.M., Navigator Green wrote in the log:

*Wind direction N.W. Wind force 6. Blowing a gale from the north-west, fine, clear, and very frosty.*

At 8:50 P.M., the *Stephano* stopped and burned down for the night. It had been a fruitless day for Old Man Kean. He had spent it picking up the odd pan of pelts, that had been scattered by the storm. But he had found no seals. Somehow, the Main Patch had vanished in the storm.

It was a bright, moonlit night when the *Newfoundland* ground to a halt less than two miles from the *Stephano*, and Wes Kean waited expectantly for his father to steam towards him with his crew. "It'll be good to have 'em back," he told Charles Green.

But the *Stephano* did not appear to be getting up steam, and Wes felt a little nagging anxiety. "Why don't he come?" he fretted. In the bright moonlight all the ships stood out sharply. Surely the Old Man could see the *Newfoundland* so near. . . .

As time passed, and nothing happened, Wes evolved another theory: "Maybe," he said to Green, "they're right in the midst of the swiles, an' Father's keepin' 'em aboard till daylight."

That could be, Green agreed.

"Just the same, 'tis a wonder Father don't steam down with the b'ys."

"Perhaps he's burnt down and don't want to move until morning," Green suggested, comfortingly.

"Yes . . . yes, that must be it." But presently he muttered, "I wish he'd come, just the same."

The handful of sealers on the ship had braved the cutting wind to come forward and gaze at the *Stephano*, just as their captain was doing from the bridge. It didn't help their state of mind to see that stretch of white, empty ice between the ships.

Wes felt the same way. Dammit! If he'd only had wireless there'd be none of this anxiety! Maybe, he thought, he should make light signals to attract the Old Man's attention. But as soon as he thought of it he dismissed the idea. Seeing such signals, every sealer in the fleet would think she was in distress. Parties would be coming from everywhere to see what was wrong. You couldn't send rescue parties out on the ice at night for nothing.

*Newfoundland* log:
   *11 p.m. Wind moderating, ice tight, and ship making no headway.*
   *Stephano* log:
   *10 p.m. Heavy NW gale continues with clear, frosty weather.*
   *11 p.m. Barometer 29.20, thermometer 9° above zero.*

With the temperature dropping to 9 and the wind blowing at force 6, the chill factor was now − 30.

It was evening before the city of St. John's began to dig itself out of the ten-foot drifts. The people there had no worries about the sealing fleet at The Front. Their concern was centered on the *Southern Cross*, now a full day overdue.

At mid-afternoon the *Eagle Point* had arrived in port, and rumours flew that the *Southern Cross* had been seen passing Cape Race. There was speculation that she had taken shelter in St. Mary's Bay. The storm had knocked out the land line to Cape Race, and rumour fed on ignorance. Before evening, however, the line was restored. The *Southern Cross* had *not* rounded Cape Race, the station there reported. She was not at Trepassey, either. The *Portia*, which had sensibly run for shelter in St. Mary's Bay, reported that the *Southern Cross* was not there, either. When the sealer had almost run down the *Portia* the day before she had been on a heading for Cape Race, the captain of the *Portia* reported.

The *Southern Cross* should have run into St. Lawrence for shelter. Failing that, she should have tried for St. Mary's. But her captain was "racing" for the honor of being first home from the seal hunt. He decided to take a chance.

No trace of him, his ship, or his one hundred and seventy-three men was ever seen again.

# CHAPTER FOURTEEN

The first night on the ice had been torture. The second was nightmare. Men lost their reason, began seeing visions, hearing voices. Some sank into mindless torpor, others went raving mad before death. That many continued to survive was incredible, but the will to live still burned fiercely in those still staggering around the ice-floes under the frosty moon. They reeled and weaved in a ghostly dance, ice-encrusted caricatures of men. The only indication they gave that their minds were still alive was when they emitted an occasional croak of encouragement to one an-other. For the most part they ignored the dead and dying, stepping over or shuffling around them as though they were lumps of ice.

Hunger and thirst increased their misery; few could have eaten or drunk without help through those cracked and swollen lips. Even those who were not dying began to hallucinate, chasing lights and other illusive visions. They spoke to their wives and children, to friends and enemies, their voices sometimes angry, sometimes gentle. Some of them wandered off to die. A few stepped off the pan into the sea, and disappeared forever. One man, driven mad with the craving for a warm drink, gashed his own hand with a sculping knife, sucked the blood, then lay on the ice to die.

Northward, the lights of ships twinkled invitingly, so bright in the clear, frosty air, as to look much nearer than they really were. A group of nine men whose minds were still functioning properly decided to leave the floe and make for the nearest ship. If they fell through the ice they would be no worse off than they already were. Bravely they started, facing into the cutting wind.

Bare-headed and frost-bitten, James Donovan plodded around the ice-floes with his young brother Stephen. Jim's hair was spiky with ice and snow, but he still doggedly refused to take a cap from the head of a dead sealer. Suddenly, as they walked, young Steve pitched forward without a sound. He had apparently died on his feet. Jim gazed at the boy, too numbed with suffering to feel any emotion. Then he knelt awkwardly, removed his dead brother's cap, and put it on his own head.

Cecil Tiller came out of a trance to find himself completely alone. He did not know where his companions were, where he was, or how he had gotten there. Food and shelter were his immediate concern. Nearby lay the frozen body of a sealer, and attached to it was a knapsack. Eagerly, Cecil opened it, and found rolled oats, bread, and raisins. He feasted on the meagre fare and felt renewed. He continued his lonely wandering, and eventually came upon a snow-lined crevice in heavy ice. He crawled into it, and sheltered there for the rest of the night.

The indomitable Jesse Collins seemed to be utterly spent at last. Though physically and mentally exhausted he had coaxed, pleaded with, and even forced less able men to live. Now he seemed to have nothing left with which to save himself. He told his friend Joshua Holloway: "We can't live through this night, Josh."

Joshua tried to croak encouragement, but presently Jesse fell to his knees to make his peace with God. Others had prayed, and died praying, and remained frozen in the posture of prayer, grotesque frozen statues. But Jesse Collins was not one of them. He rose from the ice with renewed strength, and for hours afterwards moved amongst the men, helping and encouraging the weaker ones.

Nicholas Morey, a St. John's man, knowing he was on the point of death, tried to bless himself with the sign of the cross, but could not move his frozen right arm. His friend and companion was another St. John's man, Patrick Hearn, and as Nick felt his life ebbing away he turned to Pat. "Bless me, Pat. . . ."

Pat took the frozen limb, and with fierce concentration helped Nick to bless himself. Nick then fell to his knees, mumbling, "O my God, I'm heartily sorry for havin' offended Thee, an' I . . ." With the Act of Contrition on his lips, he died, and his body remained kneeling on the ice.

Ton Dawson was resigned to death. After the *Bellaventure* had turned away from them he had lost hope, for he harboured no illusions about the fleet looking for them. His legs and feet were solidly frozen; he was unable to walk; his body screamed for rest. If getting rest meant dying, then he would die. He lay on the ice and went peacefully to sleep, surrounded by his dead companions. It was the second time he had taken the supreme risk of lying on the ice to go to sleep.

John Howlett was still watching over his friend. He had not wandered like the others, had not moved from his pan; he conserved his strength, and moved about only enough to keep himself from actually freezing. Now he did the only thing he could do for Dawson. He collected dead bodies and piled them around the sleeping master watch in a tight wall, two, three deep. The frozen bodies protected Dawson from the wind.

Howlett then went back to the sparse shelter of his ice pinnacle, his energy at a low ebb because of the exertion. Around him the moonlight shone whitely on the snow-covered forms of the dead, which looked very much like the mounds of newly-filled graves. Suddenly he remembered that he had seen those mounds before, this very scene, in fact. He was back in the middle of his nightmare, the one he had wakened from, weeks back. *It had recurred.* Now if only he could wake, he would find himself at home in his own bed. He struggled with his mind. Instead of waking up safe and warm, he kept finding himself stretched out on ice, having lost consciousness for a moment; each time, the shock of finding himself so near death restored him a little, and he struggled back to his feet.

Michael Tobin was now alone. His friend James Ryan had fallen for the last time. Two brothers, Thomas and Philip Templeman, came to themselves to find they were on their knees, shaking each other.

Cecil Mouland had not stopped moving, even once, for two days and nights. Until this night he had kept the image of his betrothed, Jessie, continually in his mind. Now he began to see other things. Once, before his unbelieving eyes, the *Newfoundland* was there, in front of them. She came towards him soundlessly, and he grabbed his cousin Ralph, shouting: "Ralph! There's our ship! There's the *Newfoundland*. Come on, b'y, let's go fer her." He came to his senses to find only the empty ice-fields around them, and the bitter wind cutting his face. Later he saw men coming towards them carrying poles loaded with kettles of steaming tea. "They've found us, Ralph! They're bringin' tea!" he yelled, but in the blink of an eye the vision disappeared. Much later, Cecil found himself and Ralph pounding on a door, pleading to be let in. The vision faded. He was pounding an ice pinnacle with his fists.

In lucid moments he said fearfully, "Ralph, we'm goin' foolish."

"Yah!" muttered Ralph, who, through the power of suggestion, had shared the hallucinations. No one had ever told them that you could see such visions without being insane.

There were snatches of consciousness when Cecil came to himself to find that he was kicking at the dead bodies of his comrades in an effort to bring life back to his feet, and in his lucid moments he looked up at the sky where the stars glittered with ineffable beauty. At least he was able to see them; he was not ice-blind, he was still alive, and from his heart came a silent prayer: "God, get me back to dry land again, and I promise to lead a better life." Inexplicably, he felt renewed.

The unspeakable cold did not relent, and the great majority of the survivors' minds were now hopelessly wandering. Men claiming they were "turning in" to their bunks lay down on the ice and died quietly. Some died sitting or standing. Some died singing. Some died walking, and their bodies froze right in the middle of a step.

The group of nine who had struck out for the nearest ship had put a couple of miles between themselves and their companions before three of them began to lag. They simply could not face the wind any longer; they were finished. They paused to rest, and died. The other six kept going.

The night went on. It was one long dirge of keening wind and unspeakable cold, and it was never going to end; it was hell; it would go on forever, and they would go on forever living in it.

Alfred and Robert Maidment were still encouraging each other to live, but as the day was dawning at long, long last, thirty-one-year-old Robert lay down and died. Alfred, unable to rouse him, crawled along the ice for about ten yards, then he too lay down to wait for death.

Daylight revealed a litter of dead men. Most of those still alive were unable to move under their own power. The dead were ghastly—the living were, too, with their swollen, distorted features and eyes that saw things in another world as they teetered on the brink of insanity and death. Many wandered blindly, their eyes sightless. Some, not totally blind, could see only a few yards.

At dawning Thomas Groves of Bonavista, who had managed to keep constantly on the move since Tuesday, stopped "just for a moment." He promptly fell to the ice. The shock of the fall woke him up and he found that he was lying across three dead bodies. He jumped up and shuffled on.

Howlett had struck the ice a number of times when he fell asleep on his feet (this was his third night awake—it was now over seventy hours since he had crawled out of his bunk) but had wakened promptly each time. At sunrise he shuffled over to Dawson and croaked his name. After much prodding Dawson stirred, rousing enough to show he was still alive, though he could not stand up.

"Me legs won't move," he mumbled, then curling himself on the ice, went back to sleep again.

Northward, somewhere on the ice-field, the bodies of the six brave men who had tried to reach the fleet lay still in death.

It was a brilliant morning. Though the wind was still northwest, and the temperature far below freezing, daylight brought hope, and even a measure of strength, to some of those still alive.

*Newfoundland* log:

*April 2 begins with fine weather and fresh breeze 4 a.m. began steaming to* Stephano *to recover part of crew which we believe to be on board her.*

This was the first time Captain Wes has recorded any official doubt about the safety of his men. His crew were ordered out of their bunks to haul coal and get up steam. He was determined to reach the *Stephano* before daylight. By 4 a.m. the *Newfoundland* was belching smoke but making little progress. She moved forward at a snail's pace and soon was trapped again. As the sky began to lighten other ships came gradually to life; the *Florizel* was already steaming, and the *Stephano* was firing her boilers.

Though nobody in George Tuff's group had expected to live throught the night, all of them did so. Tuff himself, suffering from ice-blindness, now had only limited vision. His wettings of the evening before had weakened him considerably, but he was still able to walk. Bungay and Squires were worse than he was—they were barely able to stand.

Arthur Mouland was still comparatively strong, and at dawn he was on the ice rafter scanning the horizon. He could see the *Bellaventure, Stephano, Florizel,* and *Newfoundland.* One of the steel ships, he thought, was closer to them than their own. The hard frost had cemented the ice pans together, and walking would now be easier.

He reported to Tuff: "I think the best thing is to travel to our own ship. She looks like she's froze in a pan of ice. Even if the captain isn't looking for us we'll have a chance to reach her before she gets free."

Tuff could only agree: the steel ships got away too quickly. They gathered their last resources, and prepared for that final march over the ice. Bungay and Squires could barely totter—could not, in fact, be expected to last through that interminable journey. Mouland delegated Sidney Jones to remain behind with them. "Keep 'em on their feet," he ordered. "We'll send help."

The sun, glinting on the white floes, hurt their eyes. The wind, though moderating, was still painful. They had to help one another along. Of them all, only Arthur Mouland seemed to have his full faculties. He picked the easist path between the rafters, working north and west into the open ice where they could be seen.

They were making fair progress, and were less than two miles from their ship, when Tuff finally gave out. His vision was almost gone, and this morning they had had to lead him. "I got to rest, b'ys, I got to," he mumbled, and fell to the ice.

"I want to get to that rafter there," Mouland told the men, pointing ahead. "Come on, George, we can signal from the rafter."

With help, Tuff made it to the foot of the rafter, and Mouland climbed it. There was their ship. . . . If *only* someone would look this way! But he knew their eyes were fixed on the *Stephano*. He waved, and went on waving. There was no answering signal. They would have to walk to her themselves, he thought grimly. He was about to slither down to the pan when a slight movement caught his eyes. He squinted. There, a little distance ahead, was a seal.

"There's a swile ahead," he called to Tuff—"just one swile."

Visions of hot seal meat roused Tuff from his stupor.

"A swile?" he croaked. "You've got a gaff, Arthur! *Kill it!*"

As his starving mates watched anxiously, Arthur Mouland stalked and killed the seal. Cutting it open, he took the heart and some strips of meat, and carried them back to the others huddled forlornly beneath the rafter. Dividing the heart and the meat between the men, the master watch took only the corner of a rib to chew for himself. They all ate ravenously of the raw bloody meat.

"How are you feelin' now, George?" Mouland asked.

"First rate, Arthur. I can't see much, but I b'lieve I can make it to the ship."

Tuff could still see his own feet, but nothing farther away. A man took either arm. Behind them, Jones kept Bungay and Squires on the move, but now Jones was nearly as weak as the others. When Mouland's group arrived at the spot where the seal lay, Mouland stopped long enough to cut more strips of meat from it, leaving them beside the seal, in case the stragglers might not have a knife. He then continued towards the *Newfoundland*.

Bungay, Jones, and Squires found the seal. They devoured the strips of meat cut by Mouland. Squires, who was ready to collapse, plunged his knife into the carcass and drank the blood. It gave him strength to go on.

As day lightened, the *Bellaventure* was a few miles northwest of the main body of survivors. Two men whose vision was less impaired than that of their companions sighted her and started towards her. They did not walk, but stumbled forward, reeling like drunks. The two men were Benjamin Piercey and the indomitable Jesse Collins. Behind them, a handful of survivors began to straggle along. John Howlett decided at last that it was time for him to move. There was nothing more he could do for his friend Dawson, who was still alive and sleeping. His own body was so stiff that he continually lost balance and fell and spent agonizing moments struggling back to his feet; his limbs were so "seized up" that he couldn't make them work together, but he was damned if he was going to quit. . . .

At dawning, Captain Wes Kean was in the barrel of the *Newfoundland*. He waited impatiently for it to lighten so he could see across the ice to the *Stephano*. There was absolutely no give in the ice and he was jammed again. So he stayed in the barrel, the spy-glass trained on his father's ship. Bo'sun Tizzard was in the forward barrel, scanning the *Stephano* too. As it lightened, Wes Kean could see that there was a handful of men, obviously not his, on the ice beside the *Stephano*, and that she was butting slowly through the tight ice. He did not know what to make of this. Where, in the name of God, were the men from the *Newfoundland*?

Almost involuntarily, he swung his glass around the icefield. And there, to the south-west, it caught and held the small group of men now being led by Master Watch Arthur Mouland.

He was paralyzed with shock.

These men—the thought struck him like a physical blow—had been on the ice for *two days and two nights*.

"My God . . .!"

Dazed, he stowed the spy-glass in the barrel, from habit, and almost fell down the mast in his haste to get to the bridge. His ship was jammed, but he had to make a distress signal, to alert the other ships, and bring them through the ice. . . .

He went to the chart room, found a flag—the ensign. It would not be enough. He needed a black ball to hoist above the flag. It was the international signal of distress. But the *Newfoundland* had no distress signal. What could he use?

As he gazed frantically around his eye lit upon a coal bucket. *That* was black enough, and if not a ball, it was more or less round. He seized it, staggered to the flag halyards, tied bucket and ensign on together, and hoisted them to the mast top.

This was a mistake. While the bucket would probably be recognized as a distress signal, the flag should have been flown half-mast and upside-down. And the wind turned the bucket so that from the *Stephano* it was partly obscured by the flag.

Still in a state of shock, Wes rushed off to look for the navigating officer and found him in his berth. His voice, when he spoke to the drowsy Green, was hysterical: "Captain Green . . . my men . . . something . . . *something terrible has happened!*"

Green dressed swiftly and called the steward, while the distraught captain paced the deck telling everyone within earshot that his men must have been on the ice since Tuesday.

"What are we going to do?" he cried, ashen-faced. "What are we going to *do*?"

He was in such a state that it took him a few minutes to realize he had not given orders to send out men for the survivors. He made his way to the hold, but Tizzard had already given the men there the news and they were hurriedly picking up rescue gear.

Tizzard had seen the small group of men reeling towards them descended from the barrel, and run to the hold.

"There's eight men comin' fer us on our port side. They're men from this ship," he said. "It looks as if that's all that's left alive."

"*Eight?*" It was Jordan who echoed the number. A terrible feeling deep in his gut told him that his brother and nephews were unlikely to be among that eight.

"*Eight?*" he said again.

The men had been expecting it, but the knowledge was still a great shock. They were as pale as their captain when he appeared among them, telling them to take food and rum with them. They were soon on deck, tying on their gear. . . .

Meanwhile, Wes went back to the bridge. "I've told the men to go after them," he informed Green. He stared, whitefaced, towards the reeling party off on the ice to port, then he turned hollow eyes back to the navigator.

"Take over, Captain Green," he said. "You can manage better than I can. I'm too upset to think right." He went to his cabin to try and calm himself.

Blankets, rum, food, and kettles of hot tea were passed out. Kindling was added, in case a fire was needed. Jordan, who had spent two sleepless nights pacing the hold and the deck, was still pacing.

"You'd better go with the others," Tizzard told him, as he hung back.

Jordan shook his head. "I don't think I'll go. . . ." Then he changed his mind abruptly. "All right, I will. . . ."

The small crew of the *Newfoundland* climbed over the side of the ship and began hurrying towards the eight men.

*Newfoundland* log:

*6 a.m. Some men were seen on the ice walking towards us, and assistance was sent to them.*

The entry was in the hand of Captain Green.


On board the *Stephano* the men were below decks having breakfast before going on the ice when someone dashed below shouting that the *Newfoundland* was flying a distress signal.

"What d'ye mean?" someone asked. "She sinkin'?"

"It's the men, that's what it is!" another voice shouted. "They'm still on the ice!"

Not everyone could accept such a horrible thought.

"She's sinkin', that's it," one of them insisted. This was clearly possible, in such tight ice.

But Mark Sheppard added his opinion: "I think her men have been lost."

There was a scramble for the deck, hundreds of sealers pouring out of the holds.

Captain Abram Kean was informed that the *Newfoundland* had her ensign at the mizzen peak. He promptly assumed that Wes was informing him that everything was all right after the storm.

"Raise our ensign, Fred. Let 'em know we got their signal," he said.

Then a deck hand informed him that there was a black bucket at the masthead along with the ensign, that the *Newfoundland* was actually flying a distress signal.

"We'd better make sure it *is* a distress signal," the Old Man said, then called to the deck: "Send a couple o' men across to the *Newfoundland*. Ask 'em if anything is wrong. If it's a distress signal they're flyin', tell 'em to lower it."

Two sealers hurried across the ice, and were shortly within hailing distance.

"Is anything wrong?" they shouted.

"Are any of my men aboard of you?" Wes called back. There was a dreadful pause.

"No, sir," they answered. "They was aboard Tuesday, but they left again twelve o'clock that day."

"My God! They're all lost," Wes wailed.

Mindful of their captain's orders, one of the men called back: "Cap'n Abe said if that's a distress signal ye're flyin' ye had better lower it, sir."

Then they took off, running across the ice with their ill tidings while Captain Green had the flag lowered to halfmast. Still dazed, Wes waited as the handful of survivors reeled towards him assisted by the crew that had gone to help them.

The rescuers, having met Tuff and Mouland and the others, prepared to light a fire to thaw them a little as they took a rest and drank tea. But Mouland gave them orders to track back to the three men still out of sight among the rafters.

"Bungay, Squires, and Jones are there," he told them.

They all had a stiff belt of rum, along with the hot tea, and wolfed down the food in spite of their swollen and bleeding mouths. Then Stephen Jordan anxiously pushed his face close to Mouland: "What about the men from my family, Arthur?"

"All dead," Mouland told him bluntly. Then, without waiting to rest further, he staggered on towards the *Newfoundland*. Like a man in daze, Jordan followed him.

Mouland was first on deck, climbing the side sticks unaided. The steward met him at the rail, saw the frost-bitten face, the ice-encrusted clothes, and the moleskin pants split fore and aft and at least six inches down each leg. His eyes filled with tears as he asked, "Arthur, how did ye live through it?"

Mouland did not reply. He passed on into the cabin, sat down, and ate a light meal. Then he rolled into his bunk, telling the steward to wake him after three hours.

"Have another meal ready when ye call me," he said, then was asleep in an instant.

Meanwhile, the *Stephano*'s crew of two hundred men were crowding at the rail waiting for the messengers to return. They brought the news that everyone except Abram Kean himself had been expecting to hear: "The *Newfoundland's* men are lost—all of 'em."

There was a great turmoil as men rushed into the rigging, shading their eyes against the white glare of the ice, searching for signs of life anywhere, everywhere.

The Old Man was outraged. "All hands on deck!" he bellowed from the bridge.

They assembled beneath him, muttering, and the captain roared: "Everyone who has a flask, fill it. Then get plenty o' food and blankets and get over to the *Newfoundland* to find out where the men might be. We'll try to get our ship across the *Newfoundland*, but it might take some time unless the ice loosens. Now, fill yer flasks and yer knapsacks an' get over the side!"

Swiftly they gathered spirits, food, kindling, and hurried off towards the *Newfoundland*. It was now 8:40 A.M.

Tuff, Dalton, Andrew, Russell, and Elias Mouland had been given enough help and nourishment to allow them to board the ship on their own. They were then taken to the captain's cabin where they were given brandy and more food. McCarthy and Hiscock, still together, arrived slightly behind the others. They also were given brandy and food and helped to the ship, while other crewmen pushed on to find Jones, Bungay, and Squires.

McCarthy and Hiscock were assisted aboard the ship and taken aft to the captain's cabin, where each was handed a glass of brandy. Tuff and the others were sitting at the table.

"Here's John Hiscock," Tuff told Wes.

"John," Wes Kean faltered . . . "'tis a shocking affair."

"It is," Hiscock said grimly, then added, "If ye'd blowed yer whistle, or if yer father hadn't ordered us off 'is ship, it never would have happened."

Wes, seeing the grim, accusing faces before him, jumped from the table, crying, "Oh my! What has Father done?"

Whether the captain was too distraught, whether Tuff and the others were too busy eating—whatever the reason, McCarthy was not invited to sit and eat with them. Hiscock, an officer, did not need an invitation. McCarthy did. He remained standing, Hiscock with him. Then, downing the brandy, they left the cabin to get dry clothing. When McCarthy reached the hold he was encased in ice, his cap frozen to his jacket. Two of the men, chipping away at the ice, managed to get him out of his clothes. He was given food, then crawled into his bunk, where he began to shiver uncontrollably. When the paroxysm passed, he slept.

After changing, Hiscock went back to the cabin for his breakfast. While he was eating, Jones, Bungay, and Squires arrived. Hiscock's frozen hands and feet were beginning to ache ferociously, and he left off eating to go in search of Navigator Charles Green, who had charge of the medical supplies, and who would apply gauze and Carron oil to his sores.

*Newfoundland* log:

*8 a.m. The Second Hand Tuff and some others were taken on board and reported that they, with the remainder of the crew, left the* Stephano *on Tuesday afternoon to pan seals. . . . S.S. Stephano and* Bellaventure *began searching the ice for the men.*

*Stephano* log:

*8:40 a.m. Men returned from* Newfoundland *and reported that her crew had been on the ice in all the blizzard and since 31st (of March) and be feared for their safety. Captain sent all crew in search with grub and restorative. Engineers opened ship out all she could stand to try and force to where the men were. Ice very heavy and tight packed, ship making very slow progress.*

# CHAPTER FIFTEEN

About 6:30 A.M. the barrelman of the *Bellaventure* had noticed some men on the ice a couple of miles or so to the southeast. It was, he thought, the *Newfoundland*'s crew out looking for seals, sbut it became immediately apparent that two of them (one well ahead of the other), were travelling towards the *Bell*, and he immediately reported it to Captain Bob Randell, who was on the bridge with his second hand, Abram Parsons. "Two men comin' t'wards us, sir," he said.

Captain Randell took the spy-glass and saw six or seven men appearing and disappearing among the heavy ice rafters. The two front men did indeed appear to be making for them. Abram Parsons voiced an opinion, "It must be men who fell into the water, sir." That was the only obvious reason for sealers on the ice to seek another ship.

That was probably it, Bob Randell agreed, and the *Bellaventure* kept on her course through the heavy ice, making very slow headway. But the barrelman, looking long and steadily at the men through the spy-glass, said uneasily, "There's something wrong with them men, Cap'n, they'm tumbling all about the ice."

Bob Randell took the spy-glass and observed for some minutes. The men *were* reeling and tumbling about the ice, falling, rising, and staggering a few feet, to fall again. "They must've been out all night," he observed in awe to his second hand.

Parsons agreed, "Yah! They must've."

The *Bellaventure* continued to butt through the tight ice, the ship and the lead man gradually drawing together. Whoever he was, through the spy-glass he looked to be in bad shape, and Bob Randell ordered men over the side to help him along. The second man was about a mile behind.

"What happened? Where are you from?" Parsons asked the awful apparition on the deck before him.

It was Benjamin Piercey. "I'm from the *Newfoundland*, we bin on th' ice since Tuesday marnin', a lot of our men 'ave perished," he croaked. He told them that he'd left behind fifty dead men at least.

Parsons rushed to Captain Randell on the bridge and told him the news.

"*Fifty* dead men?" the captain was shocked and a little skeptical.

"That's what he said. But he's in bad shape, Cap'n, and perhaps he's off 'is head a bit."

"That's probably the case," Randell agreed. Then he added, "At least, I hope it is."

Crew members were dispatched to pick up the second sealer as he weaved towards them. It was Jesse Collins, who confirmed what Piercey had told them. Her crew, anxious to help those still on the ice, fretted impatiently as the *Bell* made slow progress southward. Piercey and Collins were taken to the *Bellaventure*'s saloon, where an appalled young druggist, acting as the ship's doctor, scurried for his medical kit.

Hastening to the bridge, Abram Parsons suggested to his captain, "I think, sir, we should turn out all our men to search for the *Newfoundland*'s crew. We'll be all day getting the ship through the ice."

"We'll do that," Randell agreed. "Send the men on ahead."

Parsons was a close, personal friend of Tom Dawson and he was greatly concerned about him. "Can I go with 'em, Cap'n?"

"Yes, Abram, go with 'em."

Abram went to the deck where the men were already packing supplies of food, rum, and blankets; bundles of firewood they attached to their belts. "All hands overboard and do your best to rescue the lost men," Abram shouted.

Quickly they swarmed down the sides and streamed southeasterly to save what lives they could. Meanwhile, Bob Randell made his way to the wireless shack, wrote out a message, and handed it to the operator. "Transmit this to Captain Abram Kean on the *Stephano*," he ordered.

The operator accepted it and began to tap: "Two *Newfoundland* men in pretty bad shape got aboard us this morning, reported on ice since Tuesday morning and several men perished; suggest you work 'tween us and *Newfoundland*, may pick up men."

The official time of this message was 9:02 A.M.

At 9:06 A.M. Captain Randell received a messsage from the Old Man: "100 men out from *Newfoundland* since Tuesday, send your crew out eastward from you in search, captain *Newfoundland* reports seeing nine men south of him this morning."

Message to Captain Joe Kean of the *Florizel* from Captain Abram Kean, *Stephano*, at 9:08 A.M.: "Over 100 men from *Newfoundland* caught out in storm, he reports seeing nine men coming towards him this morning, all my crew gone on search, if ice loosens come and help."

Learning that the survivors lay to the southward, the Old Man ordered the Ensign on the forward staff and gave orders to point the *Stephano* towards the *Bellaventure*. His men were streaming across the ice to the *Newfoundland* in a southeasterly direction. "Go after my men and tell 'em to go south towards the *Bell*," he roared to a deck hand, who promptly scurried over the ship's side and raced after the men heading for the *Newfoundland*. He caught up, eventually, and passed the word along, ". . . Skipper says not to go to the *Newfoundland*, but to go fer the *Bell*. . . ." The order, shouted from group to group, was passed along the line and the course changed for the *Bellaventure*. Only Mark Sheppard and a handful of companions were toofar ahead to get the message, and they continued on to the *Newfoundland*.

Bo'sun Tizzard, from his position in the barrel, shouted at them, pointing, "There's somethin' on the ice . . . to the westward." Mark and his men wasted no time, they headed westward . . .

*God! What a sight!*

The *Bell*'s crew had arrived among the survivors, and their appalled eyes could scarcely believe the scene around them. From swollen, blistered faces, ice-rimmed eyes stared dully, many of them sightless from the cutting wind. The survivors were grotesque and pitiful, and many a tough sealer wept at the sight, as he hurried about his mission of mercy. Even as they were being fed, some of the sufferers expired. Pat Hearn spotted the rescuers as they came towards him, and at that crucial moment, when helping hands were reaching for him, his mind snapped under the strain of two days and nights on the ice. He wheeled and ran.

Of the men who still had their senses Abram Parsons asked, "Where's Tom Dawson?" and they pointed stiffly towards his pan. Parsons, skirting the dead bodies, came upon John Howlett, inching his way grotesquely through the snowdrifts. He sat him up, forced brandy down his throat, then food. "I'm lookin' fer Tom Dawson," Parsons said. Howlett, feeling life coming back, whispered, "Follow my tracks and ye'll find Dawson."

"Is he alive?'

"He mightn't be alive now, but he was when the sun riz. . . ."

Parsons jumped up. "I'll find him."

Dawson was still alive. Protected from the biting wind by the pile of frozen bodies, he was not only asleep, but dreaming. In his dream he saw approaching him the little daughter of his good friend Abram Parsons, second hand of the *Bellaventure*. "Cheer up, Tom," said the child in the vision. "Papa is coming."

So vivid was the dream that it woke Dawson, just in time for Parsons to find him awake on the pan.

"Tom!" said his friend emotionally.

"Me bloody legs is froze," Tom said.

There was life still in the body of Alfred Maidment when the *Bell*'s men reached him. They asked him his name and he told them. But that effort so exhausted him that he dropped back dead.

The *Bell*'s crew were shattered as the men died before their eyes. They pressed brandy to the lips of survivors and watched them die in their arms. Those already dead lay in heaps, some still in walking poses, frozen on their feet. Others were dead on their knees. Some of the *Bell*'s men were delegated to start fires; others were sent back to the ship for stretchers; those who were not ministering to the survivors were ordered to pick up the dead and lay them on pans so that the ship could pick them all up at the same time. So, like the seals they had so often panned, the bodies of the frozen sealers were stacked on the ice, one on top of the other. Many, frozen solidly to the ice, had to be chipped loose. It was grim work.

The *Bellaventure* was slowly closing the gap. Only five of the survivors had made it to her on their own, and her crew were helping the ablest over the ice, but most were stretcher cases—at best. One crew member reported to Captain Randell that he had seen fifteen dead men on one pan.

Cecil Mouland and his cousin Ralph were still alive and sensible. Cecil had to be helped by two of the *Bell*'s men, but Ralph was a stretcher case. Half-way to the ship they came across a seal. Cecil, starved and weak, asked one of the sealers to kill the seal. The sealer did so and Cecil directed, "Turn 'im over and put yer knife in 'is heart." As the hot blood spurted up, they eased Cecil to the carcass so that he could lie on it and drink. He drank until the blood filled his body with a warm, comfortable glow. Then he asked his companions to cut out the heart. They did so, and he ate it down to the last morsel. Bloodied and greasy, Cecil rose, feeling a little more like a human being.

In twos and threes, assisted by the *Bell*'s men, the survivors stumbled to the ship, thankful that their ordeal was nearly over.

Meanwhile, Patrick Hearn wandered around in the great white wilderness all by himself, blinded by the glare and glitter of snow and ice, quite out of his mind.

Message to Captain Randell, *Bellaventure* from Kean, *Stephano*, 10:09 A.M.: "Have you sent anything in shape of refreshments or spirits to perishing men?" This message had barely been transmitted when the Old Man ordered George Shecklin to ask if there was new of George Tuff. Was he among the survivors?

Message to Captain Kean, *Stephano*, from Captain Randell, *Bellaventure*, 10:14 A.M.: "Apparently Tuff started for you yesterday, men here have not seen him since, we have five on board, I think one serious case, our men report fifteen dead on pan, trust this exaggerated, but think from *Newfoundland* men's story it may be true, have sent men with drinks, blankets, stretchers, etc."

At 10:06 A.M. the *Florizel* flashed the news of the appalling tragedy to St. John's: "Fear terrible disaster; *Newfoundland*'s crew caught out in last blizzard, *Stephano* and *Bellaventure* sending men searching. *Bellaventure* found fifty men dead and dying. Ice terribly tight, we are helpless to render any assistance as yet but will proceed to her assistance first opportunity; will keep you advised to best of my ability; would advise you to intercede keep land offices open during night until search completed.* Both Father and myself in terrible way. Wes, poor fellow, in awful state. This is where wireless would have saved catastrophe if on all ships."

Joe Kean's message from the *Florizel* was intercepted by the *Bonaventure* some twenty miles to the south-east. It put the ship in a turmoil, as many of her crew had relatives aboard the *New-*

---

* The sealing fleet's wireless apparatus had such a limited range that messages had to be relayed to St. John's via land cable from offices stationed throughout the island.

*foundland*. Her captain immediately headed in the direction of the tragedy. But he, too, was in heavy Arctic ice and made very little progress.

The *Stephano*, butting laboriously southward, came across a young sealer. It was Patrick Hearn, rational now, and in fair condition. He reported to Old Man Kean that all the *Newfoundland*'s crew were dead and dying.

*Stephano* log:

*11:15 a.m. Wind moderating. Picked up one man Newfoundland crew in a very weak condition, he reported that their crew were dead and dying.*

The wind continued to moderate, and the temperature was gradually rising, but the ice remained tightly packed so that the steel ships were hard put to make any kind of headway. By mid-day, the *Bellaventure* was still labouring towards the disaster area. So far, twenty-six survivors were in her saloon, all in various stages of agony as their flesh began to thaw and feeling began to return to their limbs. Now their faces and necks rose in fiery blisters where the flesh had been frozen. On the ice, the cold had sapped their bodies; now they seemed to feel the agony of flame.

They were still coming, stiffly planting one leg in front of the other, supported by men on either side. Many were stretcher cases, but three were in no condition even to be carried over the ice, and crew members kept fires burning near them, anxiously nursing them until the ship could get to them.

Captain Randell knew well enough by now that the worst reports had been no exaggeration.

Mark Sheppard and his companions had followed the trail made by Tuff and his band. Eventually, some miles from the *Newfoundland*, they came upon the body of Eli Kean. "That's the Old Man's cousin," said one. They had no stretcher to carry the body and Sheppard, climbing an ice pinnacle, searched the immediate vicinity for more bodies or survivors. In the distance, he sighted another body, about south-west.

They hurried to it, lifted it up and one sealer exclaimed, "I know 'im, 'tis Simon Trask! He's from Elliston."

"Is 'e dead?"

"Looks like a carpse t' me."

"We better made sure."

They shook the stiffened body, calling his name, until a small sigh escaped his lungs. There was jubilation. "He's alive, there's a spark leaved in 'im!"

"We'll have to save 'im."

One man was delegated to wave a flag to notify the *Stephano* that they had found someone, another lit a fire with his greasy tow rope, and produced kindling. "Who's got rum?" Sheppard asked.

"I got rum an' molasses." One man proffered a can, its contents thick and heavy with the cold. Soon, Simon Trask was sipping the hot, life-giving drink; but he was as helpless as a baby, his legs frozen, and there was not the remotest possibility of his walking to the ship, even with help. That he was on the brink of death was evident. "Kape wavin' that flag," Sheppard ordered.

Presently, men were approaching from two directions, one from their own ship, *Stephano*, and three or four from the direction of the *Bellaventure*. Both ships were nearing the disaster area, but it was tough going.

Their own man turned out to be Second Hand Fred Yetman. "The skipper sent me ahead to find out how many men ye've found."

They told him about Eli Kean while he gazed wonderingly on the ice-crusted form of Simon Trask who still looked as if his life hung by a thread. "He can't walk, that's certain sure," Yetman observed.

It was then that the handful of men from the *Bellaventure* came to them. They carried a stretcher and immediately prepared to take Trask to their ship, but Mark and his companions had saved this man and they decided they wanted to take him to their own ship. They accepted the stretcher, wrapped Simon in blankets, and began to trek to the *Stephano*.

Message from Captain Randell, *Bellaventure*, to Captain Kean, *Stephano*, 12:59 P.M., April 2: "Twenty-six *Newfoundland*'s men aboard, ice tight, doing very best to get to them, fear from men's report at least forty men dead, am doing all possible to relieve and get to them, sent Parsons, Second Hand, out about 9 A.M. to direct our men, he just back thinks all survivors aboard here, but three too bad to move, our men keeping fire and nursing them until ship arrives, no further news of Tuff."

He wirelessed the same information to Harvey's in St. John's.

The survivors aboard the *Bellaventure* were in agony as their frozen limbs thawed, and the young druggist Harold Smith faced a battery of swollen, blistered faces, hands, legs, and feet. During his tenure as ship's doctor he had pulled teeth, sewn cuts, and treated minor burns. That had been bad enough—now this was overwhelming. But he worked on the most severe cases, lancing ugly blisters and applying gauze saturated in Carron oil.

Fortified by the raw seal meat, Cecil Mouland had managed to walk to the ship with the assistance of two men. But as he was being lifted aboard, his vision, which had held till now, began to go. Bright, beautiful spots of color floated before his eyes, and he had to be led to the saloon, where someone ordered him to lie on his back and placed two orange halves, turned inside out, over his eyes. It stung fiercely and tears streamed down his face, but the homely remedy worked, and his vision returned quickly.

The *Bellaventure* finally reached the disaster area, steaming slowly into the middle of the floes where the men had valiantly struggled to live, looking down on the pitiful shelters they had erected. The *Bell*'s crew were waiting for the ship; they had stacked the bodies on three pans like so much cordwood.

The task of loading them began, the squalling winches of the *Bell* lifting the frozen bodies aboard, and depositing them on the hatch of the forehold. Here they were laid, side by side, until they covered the hatch, then a second and a third layer, while the *Bell*'s deck hands looked on in numbed horror. The bodies of Reuben and Albert John Crewe, frozen solidly together, were hoisted aboard, as were those of Edward Tippett and his two boys, Edward in the middle, arms around his sons. They swung grotesquely in the air like pieces of sculpture, and were winched slowly to the deck, where they landed with a solid frozen thud. Somewhere in the frozen pile lay the body of William Tippett as well.

Mark Sheppard and the other *Stephano* men had carried Simon Trask over the ice, not reaching their ship until well into the afternoon. The ice was still tight but the *Stephano* had finally made it a few miles closer. Ropes were lowered to hoist Trask and stretcher aboard. It was slow going and the Old Man, leaning over the bridge, watched impatiently. Yetman had reported to him that the body of Eli Kean lay ahead, and impatient to reach his cousin, the Old Man roared, "Hurry up or ye'll lose the whole evenin' with that man."

Affronted, they speedily hoisted Trask aboard and took him below, where Sheppard and his companions had to cut the clothes from his body. Many doubted that Trask would live. Meanwhile, the *Stephano* laboured on towards Eli's body and presently sighted him. Deck hands speedily hitched ropes around the frozen body and Eli was hoisted aboard. No other bodies were sighted from the barrel, and the *Stephano* turned northward.

*Stephano* log:

*4:30 p.m. took one other (sealer) in dying condition, he was much frost-bitten, everything possible done by captain and engineers to get ship on. Doctor doing everthing possible for sick man.*

The last body had been winched aboard the *Bellaventure* and a tally kept. The last survivor had been escorted to the saloon where Harold Smith worked urgently to alleviate the agony of their burns. There were fifty-eight dead disappearing under the cover of a tarpaulin, and thirty-five living sealers in agony.

Captain Randell walked among them, mute with pity. "Can you help 'em, Mr. Smith?" he asked.

Smith replied, "They're all burned to some degree, Cap'n, but there's some pretty bad cases that need a doctor."

Randell nodded. "Maybe the *Stephano* or the *Florizel* have a doctor.

"I'd appreciate any help they can send." Smith was busily applying gauze to a blistered neck.

Message from Captain Abram Kean, *Stephano*, to Captain Randell, Bellaventure, 5:24 P.M., April 2: "I think it would be a good plan after we get all men picked up to make for *Newfoundland* and get roll called and get extent of loss."

Message from Captain Randell, *Bellaventure*, to Captain Kean, *Stephano*, 5:44 P.M. : "Was going to suggest same as we have fifty-eight dead and thirty-five alive, fifteen need medical treatment, have you or *Florizel* a doctor, our man young druggist."

The *Florizel* had worked southward all day, finding no survivors and no dead. Now, running northward again, she came upon the bodies of three frozen sealers. Joe Kean took them aboard, notified his father and Captain Randell, then began steaming again towards the *Newfoundland*. It was late afternoon and the ice had tightened when his barrelman shouted that there were more bodies on the ice ahead, but the ice had closed around the *Florizel* now and she was moving with difficulty. Up front the *Stephano* and the *Bellaventure* plowed on.

At 6:44 P.M. Captain Abram Kean wirelessed Captain Randell on the *Bellaventure*: "Both *Florizel* and we have doctors. Will give you every assistance."

The *Bellaventure* and the *Stephano*, running northward towards the *Newfoundland*, with *Stephano* in the lead, began to close the gap between them. Dr. Wallace, of the *Stephano* (a former British Navy doctor), had been notified that he would be transferred aboard the *Bell* to assist young Smith, and his medical bag was packed and ready. He had done all he could do for Simon Trask, and the rest lay in the young man's recuperative powers.

Many of the *Stephano*'s men, scouring the ice for dead or dying were converging on their ship as the day waned and were boarding her in groups. At this point, the Old Man decided to transfer the dead men from the *Florizel* to his own ship, and wirelessed Joe: "I am sending after dead men, come down towards my men, am slewing to go to Wes as soon as I can." Time of message was 6:54 P.M.

At 6:56 P.M. the Old Man received a message from the *Bellaventure*: "I think there is a body ahead of me about on our beam, if you go that way I'll work towards your men ahead of our ship."

The *Stephano* picked up the dead sealer successfully, but now snow flurries struck. Joe Kean sent a report to the *Stephano* telling his father about the bodies they'd sighted and that he planned to leave them till morning.

Message from A. Kean to captain of the *Florizel*, 8:14 P.M., April 2: "Why not put on searchlight, get them, it may be rough weather in the morning. In any case stop where you are until morning."

At nine o'clock the *Florizel* burned down for the night. On her deck were three frozen sealers, and on the ice, northward, lay more bodies. Joe Kean sent his men to the pan to stick a flag over the dead sealers, in the event that the ice might wheel during the night and the bodies disappear. His crew reported that six men lay dead on the pan. They were the six who had set out to walk to the fleet the night before.

The *Stephano* and the *Bellaventure*, slightly northward of the *Florizel*, continued to butt through the ice, trying to get sufficiently near to each other for Dr. Wallace to transfer to the *Bell*. The doctor was not sufficiently experienced on the ice to travel any distance, and it was around 10 P.M. before they were close enough for him to cross the ice with a couple of companions.

With some trepidation, Dr. Wallace began to cross the heaving ice-floes towards the *Bell*. Snow began to fall, limiting their vision, and it soon seemed that they could very well lose their way. Feeling the swells rolling beneath his feet, Dr. Wallace found himself in a strange, frightening world of which he had no experience.

But the Old Man had alerted Captain Randell that Dr. Wallace was on the way, and the *Bell*'s searchlight was brought into play. The *Bellaventure* was tightly jammed, but with her whistle going and her searchlight sweeping the ice-floes, the three men made it safely aboard. The relieved doctor and his companions climbed thankfully over her rail, and he was immediately ushered to the saloon to assist the tired young druggist.

The ice closed up. By 11:30 P.M. even the *Stephano* had been brought to a stop, and all ships had burned down. The living were again safe and sound; maimed, crippled, but alive. The dead were stacked under a tarpaulin on the forehatch of the *Bell*. The six lying on the ice under the fluttering flag of the *Florizel* would be collected at dawn when all ships would converge on the *Newfoundland* for the roll call.

# CHAPTER SIXTEEN

In St. John's, business had come to a stop, but sidewalks and street cars were jammed with people all hurrying to the cable office on Water Street. The news had spread through the town by word of mouth: "Another *Greenland* disaster."

The crowds grew until Water Street was impassable. Messages, as they came through Cape Race or Fogo, were relayed by cable and posted on the notice board. But so far they were unsatisfactory and gave little real information. "Haven't they got a list of the dead yet?" people enquired anxiously. But there was no list, and the white-faced crowd waited, quiet and fearful. There were twenty-seven men from St. John's in the *Newfoundland*'s crew.

The government, which had fought Coaker on the Sealing Bill all through the winter, had called a hurried executive meeting. Premier Morris was in England, but Acting Premier John R. Bennett invited Harvey's, owners of the *Newfoundland*, to the meeting. They asked Harvey's to order home the *Bellaventure* with the survivors, who were in urgent need of medical treatment. The owners agreed. For the first time, the plight of injured sealers had taken precedence over seals.

Doctors, nurses, and police were asked to stand by. The Seamen's Institute was converted to a temporary hospital for the less severely injured. A morgue was set up there, too. With great foresight, Dr. Cluny MacPherson of the St. John Ambulance asked for a dozen baths to be installed in the basement of the Institute, to thaw the frozen bodies.

At 6 P.M. Gerald Harvey sent a wireless to Captain Randell: "Collect all the survivors possible and do all possible for them; immediately you feel this has been done, rush to St. John's with all possible speed, with a view to saving lives; telegraph news of living and missing if without causing delay, in latter event, instruct *Adventure*. How many hours do you estimate to reach St. John's; advise soon as possible."

The Honourable John R. Bennett had also wirelessed Captain Joe Kean requesting a complete list of the dead and the rescued. At 7 P.M. he received a reply from Abram Kean of the *Stephano*: "Have two dead and one survivor, Patrick Hynes, on board. *Bell* reports having on board thirty-five alive, unable to say how many dead she had on board. Impossible to get names at present."

Patrick Hynes was in fact Patrick Hearn, but that was how the *Stephano* officers had interpreted Patrick's gasped reply to their question.

The captain of the *Bellaventure* did not reply to Harvey's. This could only mean that he was not receiving—or was already on the way home. This seemed so logical that rumors flew through the city of three ships already passing Cape St. Francis. However, at 8:30 P.M. the Fogo station suddenly came to life, spilling its clatter into the St. John's telegraph offices. A deep, expectant silence gripped the crowd as the murmur spread, "There's a message comin' through."

A voice read: "On board of the *Bellaventure* are fifty-eight dead and thirty-five survivors; on board the *Florizel* five dead; on board the *Stephano*, one dead and two survivors."

Sixty-four dead! The crowd was hushed. It was, indeed, another *Greenland* disaster, but of even greater proportions than before. The silence was broken only by the sound of a woman sobbing.

Then, shortly after the *Bellaventure*'s messsage, the instrument began to clatter again, this time with a message from Captain Abram Kean to Harvey's: "Very sorry to report worst disaster known in connection with seal fishery. The *Newfoundland*'s crew were caught out on Tuesday and Wednesday. Have waited to give you full particulars, but owing to tight ice we could not get around. Think we have picked them all up. Forty-seven were rescued alive. About seventy dead. We (*Stephano*) and *Bellaventure* and *Florizel* are all forcing our way towards the *Newfoundland* when we shall call the roll and send you full particulars late tonight or early tomorrow. The captain of the *Newfoundland* is frantic with grief. Have been forwarding letters all day to console him as best I can. Captain Randell (of *Bellaventure*) has done noble work in rescuing men with stimulants, blankets, and fires lit, and saved lives that would have succumbed a few minutes later. The barometer gave no sign of the storm."

Harvey's waited in vain for Captain Randell to reply. The executive body of the Newfoundland Government waited with them and the suspense was unbearable. How could it have happened, they asked. It must have been an "Act of God" like that which had caught the *Greenland*'s men—wheeling ice cutting them off from their ship. There could be no other reason, surely.

And where was Captain Randell?

Presently it was suggested to the Acting Premier that Furness Withy might permit them to use the powerful wireless on the S.S. *Eagle Point* with its five-hundred-mile radius, to contact the *Bellaventure*.

Capital idea, Bennett thought. At 1 A.M. he and his colleagues boarded the ship at anchor in the harbour.

What with many interruptions from ships passing Cape Race, it took hours to contact the *Bellaventure*. But finally they got through.

Captain Randell replied: "Out of touch with Fogo previous to the order dispatched for return. We have thirty-five survivors who are alive only. We have fifty-eight dead, numbers of others not yet accounted for. Fear they have got into water. It will certainly take two days under existing conditions to reach St. John's. Tell Mr. Harvey to send any further instruction by way of Cape Race."

It was 3 A.M. before dispatches were complete.

Friday dawned grey over The Front, with heavy snow flurries and raw wind from the north-north-east. The *Florizel* picked up the bodies that lay off her bow and started trying to get out of the jam. The *Stephano* and *Bellaventure* continued to butt towards the *Newfoundland*, also still jammed. It was mid-morning when the *Stephano* reached her and the Old Man climbed aboard to get the roll call. If father and son had much to say to one another, it was said in private.

The Old Man passed along orders from Gerald Harvey that all of the survivors were to transfer to the *Bellaventure*. They got ready—all but George Tuff, Arthur Mouland, and Elias Mouland. Wes needed men to get his ship in, and they agreed to remain on board.

The *Bellaventure* was still butting through the ice, and Captain Randell was besieged with urgent messages from Harvey's, demanding lists of victims and survivors, and asking when he would be returning to port. Randell, swearing at the tight ice, harassed by the messages, finally replied: "Can give nothing more definite at present as to when I may be expected to arrive in St. John's. Have not reached *Newfoundland* yet. Ice very heavy and tight, was nine hours butting yesterday to reach pans four miles away where the exhausted men were. *Stephano* and *Florizel* both here and aiming for *Newfoundland* like me. No further report is possible about the missing until I get *Newfoundland*'s roll call. Doing best possible."

This message was followed shortly by another, listing the survivors on his ship: ". . . dead unknown, not alongside *Newfoundland* yet. *Stephano*'s men report Tuff and nine others reached *Newfoundland* yesterday."

When the *Bellaventure* finally reached the *Newfoundland* around mid-day, the Old Man was there, waiting for Randell. The *Florizel* was still jammed to the southward and it seemed likely they would spend the rest of the day getting together. The commodore was even more stern-faced than usual as he climbed aboard the *Bell*, followed by Wes and his crew to identify the dead. The Old Man went to the saloon and called the roll, ticking the names as they were answered, counting the survivors against the known number of dead. At the end he announced, "There's eight men missing."

"You won't find 'em all, sir," one of the survivors volunteered. "A goodly few of 'em went foolish and walked into the sea. They'm gone, sir."

There were murmured agreements, and Captain Kean returned to the deck to begin the task of identifying the dead. The frozen bodies were identifed and tagged. Wes, horrified, was completely shattered by the sight of the ice-covered eyes of the dead and the grotesque, life-like postures of the corpses: Reuben Crewe with his son in his arms, Edward Tippett and his two sons still in a standing embrace, the other men who had died dancing, singing, praying on their knees.

At last it was finished, and the tagged dead lay once more under the decency of the canvas tarpaulin.

Returning to the saloon the Old Man made some calculations. "The total crew of the *Newfoundland* was one hundred and eighty-nine, we got sixty-nine bodies, counting the nine on Joe's ship, and one hundred and twelve answered the roll call. That means eight men are missin'. You wireless that information to St. John's. I'll make up a list o' the dead men and get Mister Shecklin to wireless 'em from the *Stephano*."

The captains returned to their own ships, and the *Bell* headed for the *Florizel* to collect the rest of the dead.

Aboard the *Stephano* the steering engine needed repairs. While this was being done the watches were alerted to be ready to continue the seal hunt. The men had not expected this. For them, the hunt was finished. They had expected all ships to escort the *Bell* to St. John's. Continue the seal hunt! What sort of man could give such orders?

The ship's officers were grimly preparing to go back sealing when Mark Sheppard, now spokesman for the men, approached Garland Gaulton. "Garland, how is it with this captain? Won't he allow you officers to speak?"

Gaulton, busy stowing stretchers, replied, "No, b'y."

The *Bellaventure* pounded her way through tight ice to the *Florizel*, took the nine frozen bodies aboard, and identified and tagged them. The eight missing men were: Henry Jordan (Stephen Jordan's brother), Mike Murray, David Locke, Philip Holloway, Henry Dowden, James Howell, young Art Mouland (probably the very first casualty), and Ezra Melendy. Out of the twenty-seven men from St. John's, eight were dead.

Aboard the *Nascopie* that morning, the crew had been anxious to learn who had died and who had survived. Each moment they were expecting orders from the owner to accompany the *Bellaventure* to port as a mark of respect for the dead. But the order did not come. Finally, at noon, they prevailed upon William Coaker to do something about it, and he sent a message to Job Brothers: "Crews fleet grief-stricken. Prospects nil. Suggest owners recall steel fleet accompany *Bellaventure* St. John's respect dead."

By early afternoon the *Bellaventure* was steaming southward with her grim cargo, heading for St. John's. It was three o'clock before the *Newfoundland* broke free and got up steam to follow. By that time the *Stephano* had repaired her steering engine and had returned to searching for the pans of seals that had been dispersed by the two-day storm. The *Florizel* was following the Old Man's lead. The *Beothic*, with twenty-eight thousand pelts below deck, wirelessed her intention of returning home with a full load.

Captain Billy Winsor was still determined to win the "race" home from The Front.

Aboard the *Nascopie*, William Coaker waited hopefully for word from Job Brothers. The crew members were restless; in the distance they could see the *Stephano* and *Florizel* steaming about picking up pans. There were no seals in sight of the *Nascopie*; in fact, there had been no seals of any account since the storm. To the south the *Bellaventure* was pushing her way through the ice, heading for St. John's, and the *Nascopie*'s crew watched her, sombrely.

At 4 P.M. the message was flashed to Coaker on the *Nascopie*. It read: "Decision as to prospects getting more seals must be left entirely to the captain. Please don't interfere. JOB."

The message was a gross insult. Interfere? He angrily wrote in his log: *"Anyone on the spot knows what the prospects are when a ship like the* Nascopie *takes 250 seals in a week, and April the 4th is reached, when every harp pupped had taken to the water. But the object of the appeal was to have the sixty-nine sealers' bodies escorted to port, in a national manner, comparable with the respect which the whole fleet consider was due to the memory of the seventy-seven men who died in an endeavour to secure wealth to maintain their country, and whose lives were sacrificed to greed for gold.*

*"Heartlessness in the extreme is the action of the owners of the steel ships in expecting men to mourn the loss of seventy-seven comrades by scouring the seas in quest of more seals, while their loved ones are being outwardly mourned by strangers in port only forty miles away, and to make the disrespect more pronounced, the* Beothic *should fly away at high pressure in order to secure the honour of being first ship to port, leaving the* Bellaventure *to creep along as she may with her sixty-nine dead forms of human freight and forty-six souls just rescued from the jaws of death."*

*Coaker* flayed Billy Winsor as well. *"The fame-seeking anxiety of the captain of the* Beothic *and the indifference of her owners for the feelings of the toiling masses of the Colony, whose sons and brothers had died as heroes upon the Arctic ice-floes in pursuance of their calling, is to be greatly regretted, for the* Beothic *at least should have been ordered to closely accompany the* Bellaventure *to St. John's and thus pay some reasonable respect to the many dead, who through no fault of theirs had been called upon to sacrifice their lives upon the frozen floe, after enduring the most excruciating torture.*

*"But even this small token of respect was denied our almost assassinated countrymen. They were only toilers in the inner-*

*most thought of the slave owners; let us take it quietly and the*
*whole thing will blow over in a few days.*

*"To the insulting reply above quoted we sent the following:*

*"JOB, St. John's: Taken 250 past week. Exceedingly obliged*
*advice tendered.*

*Coaker."*

Other ships also continued the disrupted hunt, but the heart had
been taken out of the crew, and worry and anxiety seethed in
every ship's hold. Even those who had no relatives in the lost
party felt that the hunt should be abandoned, and that the crews
should return for funeral services in the capital. Instead, they
were being sent scouring the ice for seals that weren't there. The
storm seemed to have dispersed the remainder of the herd as well
as the panned pelts.

On the *Stephano* only the Old Man was determined to continue the business at hand, driven on by an insatiable desire for
more seal pelts. Nothing, it seemed, would stop him, as long as a
seal remained alive. But now his crewmen were unhappy and the
unhappiness was producing a spokesman—Mark Sheppard. This
was Mark's first year under Abram Kean, so he was unknown to
the Old Man. But that would soon change.

The *Bellaventure* made fair progress. Bob Randell, confident he
would arrive at St. John's before dawn on Saturday, wirelessed
that he would be docking about 5 A.M., and requested that a doctor be on hand as some thirty men needed immediate medical
treatment. Three or four of the victims, he informed Harvey's,
would need carriages which could rush them to the hospital.

By dawn the streets were again filled with people who had
gathered at King's Beach opposite Harvey's wharf. The Seamen's Institute, where the victims would be placed, was next
door to Harvey's and it was humming with activity as the city's
undertakers arrived with wooden coffins, stacking them, one on
top of the other, in Grenfell Hall. The sight of so many coffins,
covered in black cloth, sent a shudder through the crowd.

That morning, too, the *Daily News* printed the list of the 173 men missing on the *Southern Cross*. It was the first official admission that she was probably lost. This meant that at the seal hunt that year 252 Newfoundland men had been lost.

The newspapers also reported that Justice Minister R.A. Squires had ordered a full enquiry to investigate the circumstances surrounding the *Newfoundland* tragedy. The enquiry would begin Monday, April 6, to allow evidence to be taken while the sealers were still in St. John's. In 1898, the *Greenland* survivors had not been invited to testify.

The morning was passing and still the *Bellaventure* had not arrived. Then a flag on the blockhouse at Signal Hall, snapped out in the wind. A ship was approaching. The crowd gathered, thickened; surely it must be the *Bellaventure*. But when the ship steamed in through The Narrows, it turned out to be the *Beothic*—the first ship into port, with a bumper crop and all flags flying proudly. No one went to welcome her, and her arrival was greeted with silence. For the first time in history a high-liner winning the sealing race was ignored. Captain Billy Winsor's action was universally regarded as a piece of callous bad manners.

A chilling north-westerly breeze kept the crowd on the move and they wandered up and down Water Street, haunting the telegraph offices and the mercantile offices for news of the *Bellaventure*. The afternoon was waning when she finally reported herself in clear water with 5 P.M. as her estimated time of arrival.

As dusk was falling, the *Bellaventure*, her flag half-mast, slipped quietly through The Narrows into mid-stream, where the port physician Dr. Alexander Campbell was waiting aboard a tender to "clear" the ship. These formalities were quickly over and she eased to the wharf.

Swiftly, quietly, the doctors, nurses, and volunteer workers boarded the ship and the injured survivors were brought off on stretchers. Their faces showed great strain as they were hoisted over the ship's railing, favouring bandaged limbs, fearful of unintentional knocks. Fatigue and exhaustion still clouded the minds of many of them. The hushed awe-stricken crowd watched them being carried across the dock. The most severely injured were immediately placed in a horse-drawn ambulance sleigh. Thirty-three men were conveyed to the hospital in this manner, including Cecil Mouland, Tom Dawson, and John Howlett. Howlett, though tightly wrapped in blankets, thought he would die of the cold on the way.

The rest of the survivors walked from the *Bellaventure* to the Seamen's Institute, leaning on the shoulders of willing helpers and hearing the sympathetic whispers as they limped through the crowd. Inside the doors of the Institute they had to pass through a crowd of weeping relatives gathered to receive the dead. It was here that John Hiscock came face to face with his father. They embraced and wept for young Joe. "I tried to save 'im, Dad, but 'e got a pleurisy stitch an' couldn't walk," John explained.

They consoled one another, while a man beside them could not be consoled as he waited for the body of his son. Nurses and volunteers, overcome by the universal grief around them, broke down and wept.

Then, one by one, from beneath the tarpaulin, the grotesque figures of the frozen dead emerged, limbs stiffly extended before the horrified eyes of the crowd. Taken to the temporary morgue in the basement of the Institute, their frozen clothing was cut away and bodies placed in hot water to thaw.

The survivors told their harrowing experiences to the press. Simply and plainly they told their stories, still bewildered as to why it had happened. They told it as they saw it. It was of little consequence to them that messages of sympathy headed by one from the King and Queen were pouring into the old port from around the world. They had been to hell and back. But in all their stories, told as it had happened, one glaring fact stood out—Captain Abram Kean had put them on the ice, miles from their ship, at the onset of a terrible storm.

On Monday, April 6, the *Evening Telegram* editorialized gravely:

From stories gathered from the survivors of the *Newfoundland*'s crew at present in the King George V Institute, it is plain the question arises whether Captain Abram Kean is to be held morally responsible for the great loss of life among the men sent out by the *Newfoundland* on March 31. Was there an error of judgement by Captain Kean who sent men away from his ship to join their own some miles away? When it comes to mere judgement by the senses as to coming bad weather, of course there is always a difference of opinion even among the most sagacious or weather-wise. But then, the captain of a ship has mechanical aid to warn him. Did Captain Kean consult those instruments and what were his grounds for expecting moderate weather to continue long enough to permit these men to rejoin their ship? How did he interpret the readings of the instrument? These are the questions that must be probed. The log of the ship must be examined for the records. At the hour when these men left the *Stephano*, the weather is said to have been threatening. Light snow was falling and the sky was black with impending storm. Is that a fact? The investigation will decide it. At noon or just one half hour after those men left the *Stephano* the storm was on and increasing in violence. At any rate that was the state of the weather experienced by the *Beothic* just a few miles farther to the north of the *Stephano*'s position. Whatever the circumstances of their leaving the *Stephano* may be, the poor fellows who were sent from the shelter of a comfortable ship have paid the price with their lives.

The Old Man, still scouring the ice-floes for seals, did not suspect the storm of national indignation that was brewing against him at home.

# Chapter Seventeen

On Saturday, April 4, the sealing crews at the ice began to mutiny. It started on the *Diana*, a small ship belonging to Job Brothers, while she was taking coal from the *Nascopie* to continue the hunt. Seven men refused duty and were put on board the *Nascopie*, since she would probably be the earlier ship into port.

The *Nascopie* was still forbidden by Job's to abandon the trip. On Sunday her men held a memorial service at the ice-field for the lost members of the *Newfoundland's* crew.

Their voices rose feelingly as they joined in the hymn:

> "Eternal Father, strong to save
> Whose arm doth bind the restless wave,
> Who bidd'st the mighty ocean deep
> Its own appointed limits keep—
> O hear us, when we cry to Thee
> For those in peril on the sea."

It did nothing to improve the mood of the men, as the *Nascopie* drifted far to the south of St. John's with the drifting ice, engaged in a futile search for seals that were now on their way back to the Arctic.

Coaker was furious. In his log he flayed the "heartless lovers of gold" in St. John's who "reaped the cream of the seal fishery" without sharing its dangers and without a trace of respect for "those who risk their lives from year to year" to "maintain them in luxury."

On the *Eagle*, one of Bowring's ships, thirteen men mutinied and were put on board Joe Kean's *Florizel*, which was now ready to head for port.

The *Stephano*, too, was having trouble. When Captain Abram Kean ordered the sealers over the side on Monday morning, a group of them, led by Mark Sheppard, refused to go. It was the first time in his life that the Old Man had been defied by a common seaman.

"What!" he roared, thunderstruck. "Will ye refuse duty?"

Sheppard answered, using abusive language, that he did not intend to go for seals for any man, that he thought too much of the dead sealers.

Captain Kean had a puritan horror of swearing. He might roar at a man until the victim was thoroughly cowed, but he would never swear at anyone, or permit profanity in his presence. Sparks flew from his flinty blue eyes as they swept the group of men and returned to fasten on the leader.

"I'll put ye on the log if ye're man enough to give me yer name," he roared.

Being "logged" meant, first, that the man would get no pay, would lose his share of the voyage. Much worse, though, a man logged by Captain Kean was as good as blacklisted. He'd have his work cut out ever to get a berth to the ice again.

Sheppard stepped forward. "Ye'll find me man enough."

Angrily, the captain signalled Mark up on the bridge and thence to the chart room.

"Log this man," he said curtly to the navigating officer, William Martin. Then he turned to Sheppard. "What's yer name?"

"Mark Sheppard."

Martin asked, "What's the offence, Captain?"

"I said that if I had a brother in the *Newfoundland* you'd see the devil jumpin' about this one's deck," Sheppard retorted. He had said more, too, about an incident earlier in the voyage.

Sheppard was logged, and the Old Man said grimly, "Well, what have ye got to say fer yerself?"

"Ye'll know what I've got to say—in the court," Sheppard replied.

"The court?" The thought of being in court had not entered the Old Man's mind. "I'm not afraid to go to court with ye."

"Ye'll get what's due ye if ye do."

For the record, the Old Man put the formal question: "Why do ye refuse duty?"

"After what I seen of this disaster through neglect of yours," Sheppard coolly replied, "I don't think ye're competent enough to look after me."

Never, in all his career, had anyone dared to stand up to the Old Man like this, or to cast doubt on his ability. Kean couldn't believe his ears.

"On Tuesday," Sheppard continued, "I asked Garland Gaulton to ask you to go looking for the *Newfoundland*'s crew—in time to save their lives."

An enraged roar came from the Old Man. "Would ye dictate to me?"

"I wouldn't wonder, sir," Sheppard retorted, "if yer career as a master isn't very nearly runned."

There was an awesome silence as Mark left the bridge. For once in his life Captain Kean was too shocked to express his feelings in words.

Later that day another gale lashed the ice-field, putting a virtual end to the hunt. Next day the *Florizel* headed for home, passing the *Newfoundland* on the way. But the *Stephano*, with the mutineers sitting sullenly below, went back to hunting seals.

Mutiny erupted on the *Bloodhound* that evening. Captain Jesse Winsor had 8,000 pelts stowed down when 90 of his 145 crewmen marched to the quarterdeck, stacked their gaffs and ropes, and announced that they would do no more sealing, nor allow anyone else on board to do it, either. The men had been given only three real meals during the entire trip. The rest of the time they had lived on hard tack and tea.

Next morning, Winsor was steaming through scattered seals. He asked for volunteers to "pick them up." When the mutineers remained adamant, he accepted the inevitable and ordered the ship to be fired up for the run home. But the crew wouldn't work the bunkers, either, and refused to let the officers work them. The *Bloodhound* drifted southward, beyond Cape Race and on to the Grand Banks, before the crew agreed to work her again, and only on condition that she head straight for port.

Early Saturday, she steamed out of the ice-floes into clear water about ninety miles sout-east of Cape Broyle and into wreckage (its drift checked by the ice) that looked like it might be from a sealing ship—gaffs and flag-poles and the like. As a result of this, the search for the *Southern Cross* was resumed in that area by the revenue cutter *Fiona* and the S.S. *Kyle*. They found some wharf sticks, some "longers" from a fishing stage, and a wooden biscuit box. The *Kyle* also picked up the floating pelts of two whitecoats, and saw some spots of oil on the water, but nothing that could be identified as belonging to the *Southern Cross*.

Meanwhile, the magisterial enquiry had started at St. John's under Judge A.W. Knight. Because the judge was indisposed, it started a day late, on Tuesday, April 7, with evidence from the captain of the *Bellaventure*, who described in dreadful detail his discovery of the dead and dying sealers on the ice pans.

Joe Kean, in the *Florizel*, made port that afternoon. Wes Kean, in the *Newfoundland*, arrived at 8 P.M. All witnesses except those of the *Stephano* were now on hand.

The survivors who were well enough to testify were called to the witness stand. Without exception, they laid the blame for the disaster squarely on the shoulders of Captain Abram Kean. They assigned a lesser degree of responsibility to George Tuff. They blamed Kean for putting them on the ice, many miles from their ship, at the beginning of a blizzard, and for not returning to search for them after the blizzard had started. They blamed Tuff for not making arrangements with Kean to have them picked up.

Tuff accepted the blame, but could not recall any instructions from his own captain to remain on the *Stephano* that night. That such instructions were actually given was confirmed by Wes

Kean himself, and by witnesses who overheard him. But Tuff, at the time, had been busy getting the men over the side, and might well have missed the import of what Wes was saying.

On the witness stand Wes Kean was hesitant and apologetic. No one blamed him very much for what had happened.

The enquiry proceeded without the key witness, Captain Abram Kean, who was still out at The Front, driving his men, trying to put the *Stephano* at the head of the list for that spring. Finally, on April 8, he abandoned the futile effort to get more seals, and headed for St. John's, embittered by the thought that Billy Winsor in the *Beothic* had beaten him that year. The few pans of pelts he had lost during the storm had placed him second.

On the witness stand, April 13 and 14, his mood was that of righteous indignation. He had done *far more than his duty*, he declared, and was now suffering for righteousness' sake.

He told his story precisely, and in great detail. It had the ring of truth. Perhaps, to him, it *was* the truth, even though many men closely associated with the tragedy told a different story.

The story he told was in sharp conflict with that told by the sealers. But he was adamant. He insisted upon testifying to courses and directions that nobody would confirm, and that, in fact, were flatly denied by almost all the other witnesses. He denied having told George Tuff that the patch of seals he was taking them to lay to the south-west. He denied that his ship had been steaming south-west while the *Newfoundland*'s crew were on board. He denied that he pointed south-west when he ordered them over the starboard side. He denied that they had crossed the bow as they left. (This would have proved that his ship lay in a more or less westerly direction.)

He claimed that they had been steaming south all the time, and that when the men were put on the ice they were near the flagpole which he had left in the heavy Arctic ice the day before.

If all this had been so, then the point where he dropped the men would have been only about four miles from the *Newfoundland* instead of about eight, and they would have had to walk in almost a complete circle to reach the *Stephano*'s flag after two hours on the ice with the aid of compasses.

There is no proof that Captain Kean lied on the witness stand. Incredible as it sounds, he may have believed that he was steaming south when in fact he was steaming south-west or even west-south-west (for, everything considered, the latter course seems most likely).* He was mistaken not only about his own ship's course and her position, but also about the position of the *Newfoundland*. She was three or four miles farther away than he thought.

This error arose from the fact that Second Hand Yetman had reported to him at 9 A.M. that the *Newfoundland*'s crew had just left her. That was when Yetman first saw them, and the rough ice prevented his seeing that they were already several miles from their ship. But, in fact, they had been on the ice since 7 A.M.

Yetman tried not to contradict the Old Man and tried, at the same time, not to tell any actual lies under oath. His position was obviously an anguished one. Is it possible that he, an experienced barrelman and mate of a sealer, looked at a ship on a clear morning and thought she was only half as far away as she was? Perhaps it is possible.

Was it possible for Captain Abram Kean to have made the same mistake, not only then, but also the evening before? Perhaps it was possible. Could Captain Kean have mistaken a south-west, or even a west-south-west course for a southerly one? Again, though it stretches belief, it may have been barely possible. It was overcast at the time and snowing lightly.

There is one really damning fact, however: The seals *really did* lie south-west of the point where he dropped the men. They walked south-west and found them, even in thick weather. If Captain Kean was telling what he believed to be the truth—if he

---

* Strangely enough, compass deviation was not mentioned even once during the enquiry. Everyone there took it for granted that they were talking about compass bearing. In fact, the compass deviation was such that a south-west course by the compass was very nearly true south.

was, in fact, hopelessly muddled about his ship's courses and positions, how come Tuff and the men found the seals?

If Kean had really steamed south, he would, indeed, have been taking the men "a couple of miles nearer to the *Newfoundland*," as Tuff recalled his having said, for the *Newfoundland* really did bear south-east from the *Stephano*. On a south-westerly (or west-south-westerly) course he was taking them away from their ship, not towards it.

There was also conflicting evidence concerning the message sent from the *Florizel*. Joe Kean and his wireless operator both testified that Captain Abram Kean had been asked to pick up the men from the *Newfoundland* as well as those from the *Florizel*. Joe then amended his statement to say this was what he had *told* the operator to send, and the operator insisted he had sent it. Captain Abram Kean and his operator both testified that the message made no mention of the *Newfoundland* or her men. No copy of the message could be produced, so the matter was never settled.

In his final statement to the court, Abram Kean insisted that what he had done, so far from being shameful in any way, was actually generous and noble:

"Now that I have looked back upon the past," he said, "and now that everything is over, I have concluded that there is only one action of mine on that day that would have saved them people from that terrible catastrophe, and that is an action of total indifference towards the crew of the *Newfoundland*. If, instead of leaving my own work at 10:40 A.M., and going and taking the crew of the *Newfoundland* on board, if I had paid no attention to them whatever, allowed them to have their long tramp for nothing, they probably would have reached my ship between one and two o'clock in the afternoon, at which time no man would think of allowing them to leave his own ship, but I acted with the very best motive and with the very best intention, as any humane father would do for his son's crew. By running back, I was lessening their journey considerably. By giving them a dinner I was strengthening them for the work of the evening. And by taking them two miles nearer their own ship I certainly thought they would have no difficulty in panning up to a thousand or fifteen hundred seals and getting aboard long before night."

"Why," the court asked, "did you not make sure on Wednesday that the men were safe?"

"Because," he replied, "when they didn't come to me on Tuesday, I felt certain they had reached their own ship."

# CHAPTER EIGHTEEN

Even before the end of the magisterial enquiry, every paper in Newfoundland was demanding a full investigation by commission into the conditions of the seal hunt. With the death of John Keels in the General Hospital, the total number of sealers killed that year (including the captain and crew of the *Southern Cross*, and the man killed on the *Bonaventure*), had risen to 253. Every major town on the east coast had lost some of its men. Of the fifty-five survivors from the *Newfoundland*, many were more or less crippled for life, and one man was still in hospital nine months later.

The "Permanent Marine Disaster Fund" was launched immediately, but out of it crippled survivors and widows and orphans were paid a mere pittance. Not a single cent of damages or other liability was ever assessed against the companies that sent the men to their deaths without proper clothing, a decent survival outfit, the food needed to keep them going under stress, or signalling equipment on their ships.

The papers were full of letters attacking Abram Kean, saying repeatedly that he had little regard for human life. Coaker, in *The Mail*, stated time and again that Kean was not fit to command a ship. A life-long Tory and former Minister of Fisheries, Captain Kean regarded the attacks as a "political vendetta," and sued *The Mail* for libel.

Coaker then went further. He published the map drawn by Captain Kean giving his version of the positions of the ships, the seals, the one flag, and the place he dropped the men on the day of the tragedy. This map was so patently contrary to the facts that it was difficult to believe it to be anything but a piece of deliberate deception, and *The Mail* flatly accused the Old Man of lying under oath.

He sued again, claiming $20,000 damages.

The case never reached court. Sir Edward Morris, the Prime Minister and leader of Kean's party, found himself confronted by writs, sworn out by Coaker, to unseat seven members of the government for bribery and corruption. Fearing that Coaker could prove his case up to the hilt and force the government to resign, Morris called in Captain Kean and asked him to withdraw his libel actions if Coaker would agree to withdraw the writs. Pressed hard by his political boss, Captain Kean agreed. As part of the deal, Coaker withdrew some of his accusations against Kean, but not the accusation that he was responsible for the death of the sealers, or that he had given false evidence.

That autumn the Sealing Law was amended to require all ships to carry wireless. It was the only result of any great consequence to come out of the magisterial enquiry.

The public commission of enquiry began to sit on November 30, with a mandate not only to investigate the causes of the *Newfoundland* tragedy, but also the loss of the *Southern Cross*, and the conditions of the seal hunt in general. It went into far greater detail than the magisterial enquiry of April, but otherwise accomplished little.

The fact that *two Stephano* flags were involved in the disaster was established to the court's satisfaction, even though Captain Abram Kean continued to insist that there was only one. It was shown that Captain Kean and Second Hand Yetman had differing opinions about the ship's courses and positions. Yetman hedged constantly, trying not to offend the Old Man—but the conflict in evidence remained.

Experienced captains from other sealing ships testified that they had "expected weather" all morning on the day of the disaster, and that the storm was actually starting by noon. George

Tuff, too, had expected weather, but testified that he was "comforted" by Captain Kean's reassurances. Like many others, he believed Abram Kean well-nigh infallible; the weather would not dare to do anything he said it shouldn't, and he trusted Kean's judgement instead of his own: "I thought the weather would turn out all right because Captain Abe Kean said 't would be fine. If he said there would be a storm I would not've done what I did."

Alick Harvey, representing the *Newfoundland*'s owners, admitted that the wireless set was removed from the ship because, in the firm's judgement, it was not giving returns for the money invested.

Asked if he had thought of it as a safety device, he admitted: "The safety of the crew was not thought of at all, or it would not have been removed. . . ."

The two commissions who first reported decided that Captain Abram Kean had been in error. He had dropped the men farther west than he intended. He had been mistaken about the flags. This, combined with the *Newfoundland*'s being much farther away than he supposed, had made it impossible for them to reach the ship. George Tuff, too, had made errors in judgement. And Kean had made "a grave error of judgement" by putting the men on the ice at the beginning of a blizzard.

The other commissioner disagreed. He filed a judgement without any apportionment of blame. He accepted everything that Abram Kean said, gave the opinion that nothing could have prevented the disaster, and described it as "An Act of God."

The judgement aroused widespread public indignation, for it was quite plain to everybody that the disaster could most certainly have been avoided. It would not have happened had *any one* of the following factors been present to upset the chain of cause and effect:

If Captain Abram Kean had known where he was, or what direction he was going;

If George Tuff had spoken up and said, "No, we want to come back aboard of you for the night";

If Joe Kean had followed his inclination to go looking for the men, instead of taking his father's word that they were all right;

If Tuff had stopped the men when they reached the *Stephano*'s flag and knew they were still four miles or so from their ship, had them dig in there, and build a really solid ice shelter while they still had strength and daylight;

If they had struck north-north-west towards the *Stephano*, instead of east-south-east towards the *Newfoundland*;

If the *Newfoundland* had been equipped with wireless;

If Wes Kean had kept his whistle blowing that night;

If Abram Kean had been even half so concerned about the men's danger as was his son Joe;

If ANY ONE of those things had been so, then most of the *Newfoundland*'s sealers would not have died.

But the disaster in that event would only have been postponed to another year. So long as the men were regarded as expendable, and the seals as the thing that mattered, it was bound to happen, sooner or later.

Still there was no suggestion by the court of any liability on the part of the company that had sent the men to their deaths. The entire public controversy centred around Old Man Kean, with the real culprits barely mentioned. Even Coaker, who had flayed the merchants in his log, fell into this trap. He concentrated on yelling for the Old Man's blood.

Sure enough, in 1915, Bowring's withdrew the *Stephano* from the seal hunt to send her on war work, and announced that Captain Abram Kean would not be in charge of one of their ships that year. Coaker was jubilant—but not for long. For under prodding from the Old Man, Bowring's bumped his eldest son, Joe, from the command of the *Florizel*, and put Captain Abram on her in his place.

On March 5, the *Mail and Advocate* published a petition signed by "fifteen hundred electors" demanding that Captain Abram Kean be arrested and charged with criminal negligence in the death of seventy-eight men. By March 8, the petitioners numbered three thousand (by March 12, the day the fleet sailed, they would number six thousand). But Bowring's stuck to their decision, and Premier Morris remained publicly "on the fence."

On March 11, 1915, Kean was awarded $500 damages in a defamation suit against the *Mail and Advocate* but this was later reduced to $100—not enough, the Old Man complained, to pay his lawyer's fee. That same night the sealers staged a mass demonstration in the streets of St. John's—a parade of almost a thousand of them, led by four hundred torchbearers, demanding the end of Captain Kean's career as an ice skipper. Some hard words for Bowring's and for Premier Morris were thrown in.

It was a brilliant and picturesque spectacle, but in the end it accomplished nothing.

Offered a body-guard to escort him to his ship next day, the Old Man refused. Hundreds of sealers blocked the street as he approached the *Florizel*. But he walked straight through them in his long sealskin coat and fur hat, nodding as he went to those he knew. They made way and touched their caps in salute. Not a hand, not even a voice, was raised against him. Whatever else he may have been, no one ever called Abram Kean a coward.

Many of the *Stephano*'s crew refused ever to sail with him again, but it did not hurt the Old Man's career. His party could not run him for election any more, but in 1927 they appointed him to the Legislative Assembly.

For twenty years after the *Newfoundland* disaster he continued to hunt seals, and in 1934 came home with his millionth pelt. He was awarded the Order of the British Empire for having killed more seals than any other man in history.

But even then fate had her little ironies. His bitter enemy, William Coaker, who had fought for the sealers as hard as Kean had fought for the owners, had been awarded the far higher honour of a knighthood, eleven years before.

# APPENDIX 1

THE MEN INVOLVED

On board the *Stephano*:

 Captain Abram Kean, the "Old Man"
 Navigator Captain William Martin
 Second hand Frederick Yetman, brother-in-law to Kean
 Cook George Yetman, his brother
 Doctor Wallace
 Radio operator George Shecklin
 Master watches John Kelloway, Abram Best, Garland
  Gaulton
 Ice masters David Dove, James Morgan
 Sealers Sam Horwood, Mark Sheppard, Dan Foley,
  Ambrose Conway, Stan Samson

On board the *Florizel*:

 Captain Joseph Kean, a son of the "Old Man"
 Second hand Nathan Kean, one of Joe's brothers
 Chief engineer John Reader
 Master watches Bob Noseworthy, John Roberts
 Radio operator Patrick Barkley

On board the *Bellaventure*:

 Captain Robert Randall
 Second hand Abram Parsons
 Doctor Harold Smith (a druggist)

On board the *Nascopie*:

> Captain George Barbour
> Observer William Coaker

On board the *Newfoundland*:

> Captain Westbury Kean
> Navigator Captain Charles Green
> Second hand George Tuff
> Master watches Thomas Dawson, Arthur Mouland, Jacob Bungay, and Sidney Jones
> Bo'sun John Tizzard
> Sealers James Evans, Eric Martin, William Lundrigan, Ariel Green, Joseph Francis, Roland Critch, John Alpheus Harris, Edmund Short, Charles Evans, James Donovan, Benjamin Piercey, William Pitts, John Conway, George Pitts, Ed Peddle, William J. White, Jacob Dalton, Frank Seward, Sam Street, William Woodfine, George Stagg, William Hickey, Frank Ryan, Tobias Cooper, William Conway, Hubert Moores, H.C. Kelloway, John Cooper, James Barrett, George Lenthorn, Richard Cooper, Richard McCarthy, Samuel Russell, Hugh Mouland, Terrence Moore, Fred Marsh, Joseph Randell, Thomas Ryan, Arthur Abbott, Lemuel Squires, Samuel Mouland, Elias Mouland, George Tremblett, John Mouland, Alfred Hayward, Thomas Mouland, Thomas Groves, Noah Greeley, Thomas Chard, Jerry Conway, John Dooley, Thomas Ring, Stephen Jordan, John Hayward, Henry Constantine, Thomas Doyle, John Antle, Azariah Mills, Joseph Rogers, George Adams, John Fisher, William Porter, James Porter, Simon Trask, Charles Martin, Benjamin Leary, John Howlett, Mike Tobin, Patrick Hearn, Mike Sheehan, Hedley Payne, Philip Abbott, Robert Hicks, William Cuff, Robert Winter, Jesse Collins, Joshua Holloway, Cecil Mouland, Ralph Mouland, Thomas Templeman and his brother Philip, Wesley Collins, Cecil Tiller, Stanley Andrews, Levi Handcock, Fred Hunt, John Hiscock.

*Died:* Patrick Gosse, John Butler, Valentine Butler, Alan Warren, Noah Tucker, Edward Tippett and his sons Norman, Abel, and William, George Carpenter, Robert Matthews, Peter Seward, John Keels, William Flemming, Simon Cuff, Hez Seward, Albert Kelloway, Michael Joy, Joseph Hiscock, Michael Murray, Charles Foley, James Porter, Fred Pearcey, Ambrose Mullowney, Charles Davis, John Mercer, Raymond Bastow, Charles Olsen, Thomas Jordan, Bernard Jordan, Peter Lamb, Pat Corbett, James Bradbury, George Leewhiting, Joseph Williams, William J. Pear, Fred Carroll, Samuel Martin, William Oldford, Benjamin Chalk, Reuben Crewe and his son, Albert John, Benjamin March, Alex Goodland, Charles Cole, Robert Brown, Thomas Hicks, John Taylor, John Brazil, James Ryan, Mike Downey, Job Easton, William Lawlor, Nick Morey, John A. Ryan, Jonas Pickett, David Cuff, David Abbott, Alfred Maidment and his brother, Robert, Fred Hatcher, Mark Howell, Edgar Howell, Aldolphus Howell, Theophiles Chaulk, Fred Collins, Percy Kean, Alfred Dowden, Eli Kean, Stephen Donovan.

*Died and never found:* Henry Jordan, David Locke, Michael Murray, Art Mouland, "Uncle Ezra" Melendy, Henry Dowden, James Howell, Philip Holloway.

# APPENDIX 2

THE SHIPS AND THEIR SKIPPERS

The Main Actors:

*Newfoundland*, Captain Westbury Kean, twenty-nine-year-old son of Captain Abram Kean

*Stephano*, Captain Abram Kean, the "Old Man," the greatest seal hunter ever

*Florizel*, Captain Joseph Kean, another of the Old Man's sons

*Bellaventure*, Captain Robert Randell

Other Ships at The Front:

*Beothic*, Captain Billy Winsor

*Nascopie*, Captain George Barbour

*Bonaventure*, Captain John Parsons

Also mentioned:
*Kite, Diana, Eagle*

In the Gulf of St. Lawrence:
*Southern Cross*, Captain George Clarke

On the South Coast:
*Portia*, Captain Thomas Connors

In the Atlantic:
*Eagle Point*